ARIZONA EATS!

BY CAROL HARALSON

RESORT GIFTS UNLIMITED
TEMPE, ARIZONA

*Warmest thanks to Ed Wade, Greer Price, Martha Clark, and Chio
Black; to all the gifted cooks and dinner pals whose dishes have
delighted and inspired us over the years—especially Harley and Pat
Manhart, and Karen Rambo and Hal Abbott; and to the many
generations of cooks we never knew but whose loving labor is the
foundation for any book about food.*

Written and designed by CAROL HARALSON

Cover illustrations and illustrations pages 4 (bottom),
11 (top), 19, 29, 37, 44, 47 by MICHAEL HAGELBERG

Manufactured in Singapore by TIEN WAH PRESS

ISBN 1-891795-06-6

Library of Congress Card Catalog Number 99-069111

Distribution rights to titles published by Resort Gifts are held by

LA COCINA COOKBOOK COMPANY,

a division of Resort Gifts Unlimited, Incorporated.

Website address: www.resortgifts.com

10 9 8 7 6 5 4 3 2 1

INTRODUCTION
Planes, Trains, Buggies, Boats, and Mules
A Bite-sized History of Arizona's Table   4

RECIPES

Green Chile Sauce 22

Sopa de Tortilla con Pollo 23

Classic Fresh Tomato Salsa 24

Red Chile Sauce 25

Skillet-Crisped Quesadillas 26

Spicy Chicken Enchiladas 27

Tomatillo Salsa with Chipotle Essence 28

O PIONEERS!

Double Apple and Buttermilk Pancakes 29

Spiced Stewed Fruit 31

Sautéed Chicken Breasts
with Lemon-Rosemary Pan Gravy 32

Apple, Raisin, and Walnut Pie 33

White Beans with Sausages and Sage 34

Chocolate Cake with Arbuckles' Ariosa Coffee 35

Grilled Leg of Lamb with Juniper Berries and Rosemary 36

ALL ABOARD FOR ARIZONA

Train Station Chicken Salad 38

Alligator Pear Salad 39

Romaine Spears with Roquefort and Apples 39

Grilled Trout with Saratoga Chips 40

PLANES, TRAINS, BUGGIES, BOATS, AND MULES

A BITE-SIZED HISTORY
OF ARIZONA'S TABLE

W HERE DINNER IS CONCERNED, Arizona has long gone its own wild way. Early arrivals called Paleo-Indians scouted up mastodon suppers with stone-pointed spears starting around 10,000 B.C. Considerably later, a new wave of inhabitants, the Hohokam, virtually invented southwestern irrigation, building the largest prehistoric system in North America to water their corn, beans, and squash in what is now the Phoenix area.

The American
Indians Native
Americans in Arizona
have ancient food tradi-
tions. The Hopi of the
northern mesas still grow
dryland corn as they did
in A.D. 1200, when Old

Oraibi (North America's oldest continuously inhabited site)
was young. The Navajo, or Diné, whose reservation of some
25,000 square miles sprawls well into northeastern Arizona,
adapted agricultural practices from neighboring villages and
sheep-raising from the Spanish. Just above the Mexican border, the Tohono O'odham, called Papago, or Bean Eaters, by

the Spanish, still harvest
saguaro cactus fruit to
make a sweet jam that is
fermented into wine.

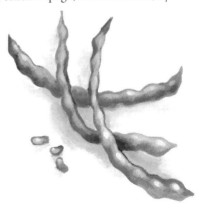

A taste of Mexico and Spain

Woven into Arizona cooking along with native foods are ingredients and techniques introduced by colonists, missionaries, and glory-seekers from Spain beginning

in the early 1600s. Spanish sheep, cattle, pigs, and European fruits and vegetables joined the native chiles, venison, elk, quail, berries, nuts, turkeys, agave, and herbs, and the "holy triad" of corn, beans, and squash, in Arizona as they had throughout Mexico, to create a new cuisine. Until 1848, southern Arizona belonged to Mexico, and for fifteen years after that it was considered part of the

American New Mexico Territory. The stamp left on Arizona's table by its Mexican heritage is as lasting as the taste for chile. In particular, the beef- and wheat-eating

culture of Sonora, Mexico's northernmost region, wafts deliciously upward through Arizona in the form of carne asada, enchiladas, quesadillas, burritos, and chimichangas. The mutton that is the foundation of Navajo and Hopi feast-day stews descends from Spanish sheep.

O Pioneers! In those rowdy decades around the establishment of the Territory of Arizona in 1863, gold, silver, and copper flowed from famously rich mines scattered from Kingman to Clifton and Jerome to Tubac. When travel was by horse and

wagon, Butterfield stagecoach, or burro in a rugged landscape over rough grooves scarcely identifiable as roads, it's a good bet that Arizona's frontier cuisine was further refined only through resourcefulness and occasional luck. Coffee, beans, venison, mule meat, and salt pork were the standard fare for

5

passengers on a stagecoach traveling five miles an hour 473 miles across Arizona.

Canned food was a blessing but a rare one. Martha Summerhays, a military bride at Camp Apache, wowed a dinner party with patties made from canned Baltimore oysters alongside the locally-procured mutton and wild turkey. Tinned fruits were such a delicacy that one pioneer's memoir records a Christmas when a can of peaches was the sole, and greatly relished, family gift.

Cow-camp cooks on the range served mostly beans, hoe-cake, and bacon. But some luckier cowhands ate rice with raisins, canned tomatoes, good biscuits, and steaks or stew from one of the beeves killed regularly and suspended from a tree in a protective bedroll to age. Most all cowhands demanded, and got, a reliably generous stream of strong, hot coffee, often Arbuckles', the "brew that settled the West" and the first coffee bean to be sold pre-roasted. Arbuckles' Coffee was equally popular on the Navajo Reservation.

Taking the train   To anyone who had jounced endlessly toward a meal of rank salt pork and mildewed beans at the next stage stop, steam train travel—finally possible in the 1870s across northern Arizona—was luxurious. Train travel coast to coast took only eleven days; the same trip by wagon had taken 166. And speed of transportation profoundly affected the frontier dinner menu, just as it has everywhere throughout human history.

Early train travelers dined where the train stopped to take on water for steam. Water tank communities were quickly tacked together along train routes to serve the central purpose of watering the train, and the distant secondary purpose of keeping travelers' bodies and souls together. For the first several years of train travel, passengers gobbled a twenty-minute meal at a shack called the depot, usu-ally rancid bacon and canned beans or maybe prairie dog stew.

Then a far-sighted English immigrant named Fred Harvey put together his experience as a former café owner and a freight agent for the Chicago, Burlington and Quincy Railroad. He had observed the traveler's predicament closeup, and came up with a system that he believed could serve well cooked meals in clean surroundings all along a train's full route. His employer turned down the idea, but managers of the Santa Fe Railway were interested, and a loose arrangement was struck. Harvey would provide the equipment and man-agement; the Santa Fe would transport the foodstuffs at no cost.

By the late 1880s, Harvey Houses were strung every hundred miles along the entire Santa Fe line and "Meals by Fred Harvey" was the railway's slogan. To serve diners at his establishments, Harvey recruited and meticulously trained a fresh-faced corps of young, single women open to a western adventure. His Harvey Girls in their starched white pinafores and long dark dresses became the emblems of a new era of western civilization that began at the (well-scrubbed) lunchroom counter. And because food flowed in a tightly controlled manner along the train line from where it was freshest and best to where it was needed, a Harvey diner in the Arizona desert could now order Nesselrode ice cream, Long Island duckling, peach sundaes, clam chowder, oysters, and mangoes, just as a Kansas City diner could. A far cry from rancid bacon and the train depot biscuits nicknamed "sinkers."

Getting your kicks on 66   Then—along came the Model T. Now you could go "off road" (which most of Arizona was) gypsying and autocamping to your heart's desire, as long as you were a pretty good pinch-hitting mechanic. Early motortouring in dusty, uncushioned, open cars was considered great adventure, and every mudhole, washed-out bridge, and flat tire became a badge of character and material for lively recollections. Autocampers fried bacon and eggs or steak and potatoes, and bought milk, vegetables, and fruit from farmers when they could. Some heated canned food, such as beans or stew, on their car radiators and ate without ceremony but with reported relish. This era may not have heightened Arizona's cuisine but it celebrated Arizonans' hardiness.

As of 1920, only about 36,000 miles of U.S. roads had all-weather surfaces, but the motorcar was already changing the nation. Trains had been a great improvement over stagecoaches, but they were coming to be regarded by some as "too soft," too remote from the natural world—and, well, they only went where tracks went. People wanted the freedom of the open road.

Responding both to need and to desire, in 1921 Congress modified the Federal Aid Road Act of 1916. The new law called for the construction of interstate highways and promised funding to states that devoted up to 7 percent of their roads to national highways. In 1926 America christened the first east-west transcontinental highway—Route 66—spanning more than 2,400 miles between Grant Park, Chicago, and Santa Monica, California.

The new highway ploughed straight across Arizona, from Gallup, New Mexico, to Flagstaff to Kingman. Route 66 meant a lot of things to a lot of people. One thing it meant to food in Arizona was a pearly strand of new eateries. The Native

Americans had developed dryland agriculture; the Spanish had brought pigs and sheep; the trains had inspired mud-shack meals and then sparkling Harvey Houses; now the Mother Road brought roadside cafés, Mom-and-Pop restaurants, and, finally, fledgling franchises.

Eventually the same road would carry artichokes from California past the back fences of Flagstaff to New Jersey, and oranges from Florida to Kingman. "Homemade" was the hallmark of the early eateries on 66—even when "home" was a six-booth, plank-floored coffee shop. In Arizona, homemade

meant meals with the heart of that ancient native staple, corn, the spice of the Southwestern chile, the mark of the Spanish friar, the ingenuity of the pioneer.

Running the rivers   Since the first exploration of the Colorado River deep in the great chasm of the Grand Canyon in 1869 by a one-armed Civil War veteran named John Wesley Powell, Arizona rivers have held profound fascination for adventurers.

These days, the rite of passage along the steep-walled canyon rivers of the state is undertaken regularly by groups of

9

intrepid boatmen. Travelers sign on for trips of a few days to
two or three weeks. The subculture of river guides and regular
river sojourners is an important part of Arizona culture. And
an important part of the river trips is the food. River cooks
bring whole collapsible kitchens along by boat, with all the
food that will be needed for up to two dozen hungry, sun-
burned pilgrims who have been paddling through rapids all
day. It's a vigorous art, this riverside cooking and, like the best
chuckwagon "Cookies," the great river cooks are legend.

The new Southwestern table

Food in Arizona. It has
been transported by Indians on foot,
by settlers with mule and wagon, by
Model T, in waterproof packets
down white-churning rivers.
Eventually it flew through the air.
When air travel, air transport, and
new technologies for storage and
preservation became available,
Arizona, as elsewhere, gained the glory of seacoast riches one

day out of the water, spices harvested last week in Africa, asparagus and strawberries in January. An indulgent blessing, but a blessing.

The "new Southwestern cooking" combines native ingredients, Hispanic inspiration, cowboy flavors, culinary traditions from many far-flung places, and local and exotic foodstuffs in a blend that is hard to describe but recognizably contemporary. French techniques marry Mexican chiles; chuckwagon beans meet Asian spices; the explorer's adventure has moved to the kitchen and the stove is the new frontier.

Though inspired by the larder of history, the recipes that follow are designed to please contemporary tastes (no beef hung in a bedroll to dissuade the coyotes). Wherever your table is set, may you have a Model T autocamper's resourcefulness and zest, a Santa Fe Railway passenger's sense of luxury, and the appetite and good company of an early-day Route 66'er. Happy eating!

AMERICAN INDIAN WAYS

I t's no secret that the first Americans were also the first cooks on the continent and that thousands of years before the appearance of Europeans they were studying the natural larder of the Southwest. From their long experience, and from the possibilities of the land, came our acquaintance with many wild foods: piñon nuts, sunflower seeds, black walnuts, berries. In general, the longer a tribe inhabited a given area, the more deeply they came to know its resources. The Hopi, who have been on their land perhaps longer than any other native tribe, use virtually every wild plant that grows there.

The desert is a tough-love landscape. When agriculture developed in prehistoric Arizona, it demanded ingenious dry-land farming techniques. At a time (the fifteenth and six-teenth centuries) when European farmers were broadcasting seed by the handful and then laboriously weeding back to the desired plant, American Indians were growing corn, beans, and squash methodically in orderly rows. Corn, in particular, was key to life.

The word *corn* in English means "staple grain." Wheat, oats, or rye were "corn" to Europeans if they were the mainstay of the people. When Europeans arrived in America, they saw Indians cultivating, revering, and nourishing themselves with a strange giant grass that bore its seeds in neat rows enclosed within package-like husks. They called it corn. Native speakers called it Mother, Life, or She Who Sustains Us. At some time in the long-distant past, in some way we still do not understand, Indian farmers had bred a self-sowing ancient grass with tiny edible grains into a tall, proud plant with huge kernels that must be sown by human hand as it cannot sow itself from seed.

We associate this gift of Native America with succulent roasting ears

enjoyed at the height of summer. But its presence in our lives is actually almost as prevalent as it was in the lives of ancient Indians. Cornstarch is used in everything from baby food to yeast to headache tablets and match heads. Corn syrup gives body to ketchup and ice cream, soups, and sauces; nearly all adhesives contain corn; canned foods are bathed in a liquid containing corn; food packaging is partly made of corn. Even meat, butter, milk, and eggs are, essentially, corn, since that's largely what sustains all those cows and chickens.

The blue corn developed by the Hopi Indians of what is now Arizona has over 20 percent more protein than white flour, and more minerals. The Hopi still make their ancient earth-perfumed, paper-thin scrolls of blue-corn piki bread for all special occasions.

PIKI BREAD

3 to 4 cups finely-ground blue cornmeal
3 tablespoons ashes of the four-wing saltbush
1/2 cup boiling water plus lukewarm water
Piece of sheep's spinal cord
Piece of sheep's skin or clean cloth

Combine 1/2 cup boiling water with the ashes and set aside. Place the cornmeal in a large bowl and make a well in the center. Strain the water from the ashes and add to the bowl. Add additional water and stir to make a thin batter. Mix until smooth. Heat the piki stone (a special stone used for making piki). Rub it with a piece of sheep's spinal cord.

Spread a small portion of batter across the hot stone to bake. The sheet of piki will be fragile and as thin as a piece of tissue paper. Peel from the stone. Wipe the stone with more batter for a second piki. Lay the previous piki on top of the one baking on the stone so the steam will soften it enough to roll it up. Place pikis in a flat basket tray as they are baked. Always feed the first piki to the fire.

From time to time, scrape the stone with the sheepskin or cloth and rub it with the spinal cord.

Hopi maidens traditionally were expected to become adept at the difficult art of piki making. When a girl decided on her chosen sweetheart, she took a basket of piki to his family's door at night. If the basket had been gathered in by morning, the pair was betrothed. The girl then went to her future husband's home to grind corn "to pay for the boy" while the boy's male relatives wove her wedding garments.

Blue Corncakes with Mesquite Honey Butter

Chio Black of Sedona makes these nutritious pancakes with blue cornmeal from the Hopi Reservation, where she grew up. The basic dry mix will keep for months. Add blueberries or other fruit if you like, and serve with Honey-Butter (below) or Apple Topping (page 30) and smoky bacon.

FOR THE DRY MIX:

2 CUPS BLUE CORNMEAL

1/2 CUP EACH OAT BRAN, WHEAT BRAN, WHEAT GERM

1/2 CUP SESAME SEEDS (OPTIONAL)

FOR SIX CORNCAKES:

1 CUP DRY MIX (SEE ABOVE)

3/4 TEASPOON BAKING POWDER

APPROXIMATELY 1/2 CUP MILK

1 EGG WHITE

1/4 CUP CHOPPED WALNUTS OR PECANS

HONEY-BUTTER FOR SIX CORNCAKES:

1/2 TO 3/4 CUP MESQUITE HONEY, OR A QUANTITY
TO TASTE

1/4 CUP MELTED BUTTER

Combine the ingredients for the dry mix and store in a tightly closed container in a cool place.

When you're ready to make corncakes, combine 1 cup mix with 3/4 teaspoon baking powder. Add enough milk to create a thin batter. Beat the egg white to soft peaks and fold into the batter. Fold in nuts and berries, if desired.

Heat a heavy, large skillet and add a little butter or oil, or coat with cooking spray. Ladle a portion of batter into the skillet for each cake. Pancakes are easier to handle if you make them relatively small, about 4 inches or a bit more in diameter. Cook the cakes until they are dark golden brown, flipping once when bubbles begin to appear in the batter.

Blend honey and butter and drizzle over, or cover with maple syrup and warmed homemade preserves or other favorite toppings.

Bacon Biscuits with Piñon Nuts

Piñon pines flourish in the Piñon-Juniper belt (from 4,500 to 6,500 feet) of the Arizona uplands. The sweet, oil-rich nuts have been shaken from the cones of PINUS MONOPHYLA for food in the Southwest for centuries. Serve these biscuits with stew, toast them topped with cheese for a light supper, or smother with creamed chicken. Split, butter, and toast leftover biscuits for breakfast. Makes 8 to 10 large biscuits.

1 PACKET (1 1/4 TEASPOONS) FAST-ACTING DRIED YEAST SUCH AS RED STAR RAPIDRISE

5 TABLESPOONS WARM WATER

3 TABLESPOONS SUGAR

2 CUPS BUTTERMILK, AT ROOM TEMPERATURE

2/3 CUP VEGETABLE OIL OR CANOLA OIL, SCANT

4 1/2 TO 5 CUPS ALL-PURPOSE UNBLEACHED FLOUR

5 TEASPOONS BAKING POWDER

1 TEASPOON BAKING SODA

2 TEASPOONS KOSHER SALT

1/2 CUP PIÑON NUTS, TOASTED IN A DRY SKILLET

7 STRIPS LEAN BACON, FRIED, DRAINED, CRUMBLED

MILK OR CREAM MIXED WITH BEATEN EGG FOR GLAZE

Put yeast in a medium-sized mixing bowl and add water. Stir to dissolve yeast. Stir in sugar, buttermilk, and oil (the mixture will not blend; oil will float on top).

Combine flour, baking powder, baking soda, and salt in a large mixing bowl and whisk to blend and aerate.

Pour the yeast-buttermilk mixture into the bowl full of dry ingredients. Stir just to moisten. Turn out onto a board and knead 5 to 6 strokes. Pat into a ball and place in a bowl, covered with a clean cloth, in a warm place for 30 minutes, or longer if more convenient. (You can also refrigerate at this stage for up to a day.)

Roll out the dough. Sprinkle with half the piñon nuts and bacon. Fold over in half, and roll out again to a thickness of about one-half inch. Repeat with remaining nuts and bacon. Cut into rounds with a biscuit cutter or coffee cup and place the rounds on a buttered baking sheet 1 1/2 inches apart.

Place the baking sheet in a *cold* oven and set the temperature at 450° (biscuits will rise and bake as the oven heats.) Bake 10-15 minutes, or until biscuits are almost done. Remove from oven and brush lightly with milk or cream (beaten with an egg, if desired). Return to oven and bake 2 to 3 minutes more, or until puffy, golden, and glazed.

Fresh Corn and Sage Muffins

Semolina is flour made from durum wheat, a hard wheat that is very high in protein and therefore yields lots of gluten. Gluten is the elastic substance formed when two proteins in wheat flour are combined with water. These proteins weave themselves together and trap air bubbles when the batter is baked, causing the muffins to rise nicely. Serve these quick muffins with roast turkey, baked or sautéed chicken breasts (page 32), or vegetable soup. Makes 8 to 10 large muffins.

1 CUP ALL-PURPOSE UNBLEACHED FLOUR

1/2 CUP SEMOLINA FLOUR

1/2 CUP STONE-GROUND CORNMEAL

3 TABLESPOONS BAKING POWDER

4 TABLESPOONS SUGAR

1 1/4 TEASPOONS KOSHER SALT

2 LARGE EGGS

3/4 CUP MILK, AT ROOM TEMPERATURE

1/4 CUP MELTED BUTTER OR MARGARINE, AT ROOM
    TEMPERATURE

1/4 CUP BUTTERMILK, AT ROOM TEMPERATURE

2 TO 3 LARGE FRESH SAGE LEAVES, CHOPPED, OR 1
TEASPOON DRIED CRUMBLED SAGE LEAVES
CORN KERNELS CUT FROM ONE EAR OF BOILED OR
ROASTED CORN ON THE COB (ABOUT 3/4 CUP)
CRACKED BLACK PEPPER

Preheat the oven to 425°. Place the flours, cornmeal, baking powder, sugar, and salt in a large mixing bowl and whisk to blend.

In a separate bowl, beat the eggs. Add the milk, butter, and buttermilk and beat to blend.

Pour the milk mixture into the flour mixture and stir just to moisten (overmixing will make the muffins tough). Gently fold in the sage, corn, and cracked black pepper.

Spoon the batter into oiled, buttered, or cooking-spray coated baking cups.

Bake 20 minutes or until puffed and golden.

Posole with Oxtails

You may have to ask the butcher at your supermarket for oxtails if they are not in the meat case, but it's worth the trouble. Oxtails make the richest, clearest, best flavored beef broth. Posole is large-kerneled hominy corn presoaked in water and unslaked ground limestone, a naturally occurring mineral. Lime serves the same purpose as four-winged salt-bush ash in Hopi blue corn preparation. In addition to soft-ening the outer skin for easier grinding, this alkali source releases the bound vitamin niacin, making it available to the human body. Without this step, corn alone could never have been the central support for human life.

Look for limed posole in the meat case or Hispanic section of your supermarket. Serve with flour tortillas rolled around salsa and cheese and heated through. Serves 8.

1 1/2 POUNDS OXTAILS

1 TABLESPOON OLIVE OIL

1/2 WHITE ONION, PEELED AND CHOPPED

2 CLOVES GARLIC, SMASHED, PEELED, CHOPPED

1 TABLESPOON CUMIN SEEDS, TOASTED IN A DRY
SKILLET AND GROUND, OR GROUND CUMIN

1 BAY LEAF

1 TABLESPOON CRUMBLED DRIED SAGE LEAVES

1 TABLESPOON DRIED MEXICAN OREGANO

1 1/2 TEASPOONS KOSHER SALT

1/2 TEASPOON FRESHLY CRACKED BLACK PEPPER

1 SMALL HOT DRIED CHILE, CRUMBLED (MORE TO TASTE)

3 CUPS POSOLE (UNCOOKED LIMED HOMINY CORN, ALSO CALLED NIXTAMAL) RINSED IN A COLANDER AND DRAINED

Rinse the oxtails and put them in a large stewpot. Cover with water by four inches and bring to a boil. Meanwhile, in a separate large heavy pot, sauté the onion in the olive oil. When nearly soft, add the garlic and sauté 3 minutes. Add the cumin, bay leaf, sage, oregano, salt, pepper, and crushed chile. As you are doing this, watch the oxtail broth in its separate pot, continuing occasionally to skim off the foam that will rise to the surface. When the oxtail broth is clear, remove the oxtails to the stewpot with the onion mixture. Strain in the liquid from the oxtails. Add the posole and continue to cook at a rapid simmer 3 hours or more, until the posole and meat are tender. Remove the oxtails and shred the meat from them. Return the meat to the pot and heat through.

Honeyed
Butternut-Squash Pie

Squash has been grown in Arizona for thousands of years.
When the Europeans arrived with new varieties, American
Indians in the area simply added the imports to their squash
repertoire. This succulent dessert pie—something like sweet
potato pie—serves 8.

1 1/4 CUPS UNBLEACHED ALL-PURPOSE FLOUR

1/2 TEASPOON KOSHER SALT

1 STICK (1/2 CUP) UNSALTED BUTTER, COLD, IN BITS

4 TABLESPOONS ICE WATER

2 TO 2 1/2 POUNDS BUTTERNUT SQUASH

2 TABLESPOONS BUTTER, AT ROOM TEMPERATURE

3 TABLESPOONS UNSULPHURED MOLASSES

2 TABLESPOONS FRESHLY-SQUEEZED LEMON JUICE

1/2 TO 3/4 CUP DARK BROWN SUGAR, PACKED

1/4 CUP HONEY

3 LARGE EGGS

1/2 CUP HEAVY CREAM

1/2 TEASPOON EACH GROUND NUTMEG AND GINGER

1 TEASPOON GROUND CINNAMON

1/2 TEASPOON KOSHER SALT

Place the flour and salt in a food processor and whirl to blend. Add the butter and pulse several times, until the butter is cut into the flour and the mixture has a coarse sandy texture. Add the water. Whirl until the dough forms a ball, about one minute. Remove from the food processor, wrap in plastic wrap, and chill one hour.

While the dough ball is chilling, bake the squash. Slice squash in half and spoon out the seeds. Score lightly and spread with butter. Drizzle with molasses and lemon juice. Place in a parchment- or foil-lined baking pan and bake at 400° for 45-60 minutes or until the flesh is tender. Remove squash and lower the oven to 375°. When the squash is cool enough to handle, peel the skins off and chop the flesh into a large bowl or a food processor bowl. Mash by hand with a potato masher, or whirl in food processor until creamy and smooth—you should have approximately 3 1/2 cups of purée. Roll out the pie dough on a floured board and fit into an unbuttered pie pan. Return to the refrigerator to keep chilled.

Combine the pureéd squash with the brown sugar, honey, eggs, cream, spices, and salt. Pour into the pie crust. Bake on the lowest rack in the oven 50 to 60 minutes. Remove from the oven when the filling is puffy and well set but still visibly moist in the center.

The Famous
Navajo Taco

*Fry bread, the foundation for the Navajo Taco, is some-
thing like a Mexican sopapilla. Served with a dusting of cinnamon and sugar, it's breakfast on the Reservation.
Smothered with chile and cheese to make a Navajo Taco, it's
familiar festival food, sold from a portable food stall at every
special event or celebration. Serve fry bread fresh and hot,
immediately after making it, for the best texture. Serves 4.*

3 TABLESPOONS SOFTENED BUTTER OR SHORTENING

2 1/4 CUPS ALL-PURPOSE FLOUR (NAVAJOS SWEAR BY
BLUEBIRD FLOUR FOR FRY BREAD)

2 TEASPOONS BAKING POWDER

1 TEASPOON SALT

1 CUP LUKEWARM WATER (APPROXIMATE)

OIL FOR DEEP FRYING (8 TO 10 CUPS VEGETABLE
SHORTENING SUCH AS CRISCO, OR LARD, IS
TRADITIONAL)

TEXAS-STYLE CHILE MADE WITH MEAT AND BEANS

GRATED CHEDDAR CHEESE

SHREDDED LETTUCE

SALSA

Melt 2 tablespoons of the shortening and set aside. Combine flour, baking powder, and salt in a large mixing bowl. Add the remaining tablespoon of butter or shortening and rub it into the flour with your fingertips as for pie crust. Add the water slowly, starting with about one-half cup, and mix until the dough is soft but not sticky (you may need slightly more or less than 1 cup water). Turn the dough out onto a board and knead 6 to 8 strokes. Quarter the dough and form into 4 balls. Coat each with the softened butter or shortening. Let dough balls stand 25 minutes to relax the gluten.

Heat the oil in a deep, large, heavy iron skillet, preferably cast-iron, to about 375° or until a small pinch of dough added to the oil browns in about a minute.

While the oil is heating, roll out the dough balls into flat disks, using your hands or a rolling pin. Prick each several times with a fork. Fry the breads one at a time till golden and puffy, turning once after bubbles appear on the first side. Drain well on paper towels.

Top each fry bread with heated chile, cheese, and lettuce, and serve immediately with salsa alongside.

A TASTE
OF MEXICO AND SPAIN

The second group of people to see Arizona, after the American Indians, whose home it had long been, were the Spanish.

In theory, at least, Arizona was part of the New Spanish Empire in the fifteenth century. In reality, as it had been so little explored, the Spanish government based in Mexico City referred to it as the "northern mystery."

In the mid-1500s several small waves of Spanish explorers crossed upwards into Arizona, herding their cattle, sheep, and pigs for food along the way. None found the fabled golden cities that legend told of; many met privation and some met death. The final waves of Spanish immigrants were mostly Franciscan missionaries, and in 1629 they established a mission among the Hopi near Awatovi. The great Pueblo revolt of 1680, however, forced them out. From then on, Spanish mission activity was focused in southern Arizona.

In 1775 the garrison at Tubac was moved to an Indian village renamed by the Spanish San Agustín del Tucson. In this melting pot of Spanish and Indian cultures, life carried on while Mexico went through the upheavals that eventually led to establishment of the Republic of Mexico. Mexico sold the area to the United States as part of the Gadsden Purchase towards the end of the 19th century, but the Spanish legacy of the early days lives on. Nearly 20 percent of Arizona's population is of Spanish descent, and Spanish culture and cuisine—often wed to indigenous Indian culture, as it is throughout Mexico—continue to enrich the Arizona table, especially in the south.

For Arizona cooking, this means that chimichangas and enchiladas are on almost as many menus as cheeseburgers and omelettes. It also has helped establish a conduit for that magnificent seasoning staple of Mexican food, the chile pepper, to enter the cooking styles of modern Arizonans. Chile flavors show up (and show off) in everything from soup to nuts.

19

Carne Asada
(Marinated Grilled Skirt Steak)

From northern Mexico came carne asada ("grilled meat"). Skirt steak, the traditional meat for this dish, is the well-marbled diaphragm muscle of the beef. It is most tender when sliced thinly diagonal to the grain after cooking. This version of the dish is not completely traditional, but it's delicious. Serve with Garlicky Smashed Potatoes (page 57) or tortillas, roasted sweet red peppers, and diced avocado with a squeeze of fresh lime juice. Serves 4.

1/2 CUP MEXICAN BEER

1/2 CUP BEEF BROTH

1/2 YELLOW ONION, PEELED AND MINCED

3 TABLESPOONS DARK BROWN SUGAR (PACKED)

1 TEASPOON CRUMBLED DRIED MEXICAN OREGANO

3 TABLESPOONS WORCESTERSHIRE SAUCE

2 TABLESPOONS BALSAMIC VINEGAR

1 TABLESPOON CUMIN SEEDS, TOASTED IN A DRY SKILLET AND GROUND OR POUNDED IN A MORTAR

3 CLOVES GARLIC, PEELED, SMASHED WITH THE BACK
   OF A KNIFE, CHOPPED
3 TABLESPOONS OLIVE OIL
1 1/2 POUNDS SKIRT STEAK
KOSHER SALT AND CRACKED BLACK PEPPER

Combine beer and broth in a saucepan and cook rapidly until reduced to about 1/4 cup liquid. Pour into a glass bowl and stir in the remaining ingredients except steak, salt, and pepper, to make a marinade. Place the steak in a sealable plastic bag and pour the marinade over it. Close the bag tightly and massage the meat to begin the marination. Place the bag in a large shallow bowl in case of leaks and marinate, refrigerated, about two to three hours, turning occasionally. Remove steak from marinade and rub both sides generously with salt and pepper.

Fire up the grill to high, using natural charcoal. To add a smoky flavor, toss a handful of soaked and drained apple or hickory chips into the coals just before placing the steak on the grill. Cook over direct heat approximately 4 minutes per side for rare meat (it should register 140° on a meat thermometer when cooked rare) or to taste. Let stand 5 minutes before slicing thinly against the grain of the meat.

Green Chile and
Roasted Red Pepper Tamales

Masa is limed hominy corn kernels ground to a dough-like paste — grainy and corn-fragrant. Find it in the meat section of the market, or with Hispanic foods. You can sometimes get it from good Mexican restaurants too. Serve with Red or Green Chile Sauce or salsa (pages 22, 25, 28).

2 CUPS SHREDDED SHARP CHEDDAR CHEESE

2 CUPS SHREDDED MONTERREY JACK CHEESE

3 POBLANO CHILES

4 TO 5 ANAHEIM (LONG GREEN) CHILES

KERNELS SLICED FROM 2 BOILED OR ROASTED EARS OF CORN, SEASONED WITH BUTTER AND SALT (ABOUT 3/4 CUP)

1 WHITE ONION

5 POUNDS MASA

3 TEASPOONS KOSHER SALT

1-1/2 TEASPOONS BAKING POWDER

1/2 POUND BUTTER

1/3 POUND VEGETABLE SHORTENING

1-1/2 CUPS GOOD CHICKEN BROTH

Prepare the fillings: Mix the two cheeses in a bowl and set aside. Roast the chiles over the flame of a gas burner or under a hot broiler until they are charred on all sides. Remove with tongs to a plastic bag and fold closed. When they have cooled, peel and seed them and cut them into strips. Prepare the corn kernels. Peel and chop the onion.

Soak the corn husks in hot water.

Put the masa in an electric mixer bowl (it may be necessary to make the tamale dough in two batches). Add salt, baking soda, butter, and shortening. Beat to blend. Add the broth a small amount at a time. Keep mixing at high speed between additions. The object is to arrive at a creamy, moist, fluffy batter about the consistency of whipped butter. Test it for lightness by dropping a pinch of dough into a glass of cold water. If it floats to the top, the dough is light enough.

Drain the corn husks and pat dry.

Smear one (or two overlapping, if they are smaller) husks with a heaping tablespoonful or two of tamale dough. In the center of the thick smear of tamale dough, put filling (2 or 3 strips of chile, 2 or 3 tablespoons of cheese, a sprinkling of corn kernels and chopped onion).

Hold the husk by both sides, lengthwise, and shake it a little while rolling it shut from both sides in order to enclose the filling inside the smear of dough. Close both ends by tying them shut with strips of corn husk. Continue making tamales until the filling and dough are all used.

At this point you can refrigerate the tamales in a sealable plastic bag for up to 2 days, if desired.

To steam the tamales: Layer them in the top of a deep steamer and steam about an hour. To check for doneness, remove one and open it a little bit. If the dough pulls away from the husk, it's done. Don't overcook or tamales will not be moist and tender.

Green Chile Sauce

This classic is great on enchiladas, tamales, quesadillas, or scrambled eggs, or dolloped atop a bowl of chile or tortilla soup. Serves 4 as a sauce or garnish.

1 SMALL ONION, CHOPPED

1 TABLESPOON OLIVE OIL

1 GARLIC CLOVE, PEELED, SMASHED, AND CHOPPED

8 ANAHEIM (LONG GREEN) CHILES, ROASTED, SEEDED,
   PEELED, CHOPPED

1 DRIED CHIPOTLE CHILE, SCRUBBED, SOAKED IN
   BOILING WATER, SEEDED AND CHOPPED (OPTIONAL)

1/2 TEASPOON GROUND CUMIN OR CUMIN SEED
   TOASTED IN A DRY SKILLET AND GROUND

1/2 TEASPOON CRUMBLED DRIED OREGANO

1/2 CUP CHICKEN BROTH

1 TEASPOON CORNSTARCH

2 TEASPOONS COLD WATER

1/2 TEASPOON SUGAR

1/2 CUP CILANTRO SPRIGS

KOSHER SALT AND CRACKED BLACK PEPPER TO TASTE

Brown the onion in the oil. When beginning to color, add garlic. Add spices and chiles. Cook 2 to 3 minutes till spices are aromatic. Add broth and cook 20 minutes. Cool slightly and remove to a food processor or blender. Whirl just until slightly blended (leave the mixture coarse in texture) and return to the saucepan. Mix cornstarch and water and add to the pan. Cook 10 minutes. Stir in sugar, cilantro, salt, and pepper, and correct seasonings.

Sopa de Tortilla con Pollo

Tortilla soup was likely devised as a tasty way to make a meal of day-old tortillas. As with European country soups, every cook has a favorite version. This one—"con pollo," or "with chicken"—is enriched with white meat of chicken. Cut the ingredients into generously chunky pieces for the satisfying texture of a meal in a bowl. Serves 6.

12 STALE CORN TORTILLAS, CUT INTO WIDE STRIPS

VEGETABLE OIL OR PEANUT OIL FOR FRYING TORTILLA STRIPS

6 TO 8 SPLIT CHICKEN BREASTS

4 TO 5 CUPS HOMEMADE OR GOOD QUALITY COMMERCIAL CHICKEN BROTH OR STOCK

1 TEASPOON KOSHER SALT

1 TABLESPOON CUMIN SEED, TOASTED IN A DRY SKILLET AND GROUND, OR GROUND CUMIN

1 TABLESPOON DRIED MEXICAN OREGANO

1 TEASPOON DRIED THYME (PREFERABLY LEMON THYME) OR ONE TEASPOON SNIPPED FRESH THYME

2 SMALL YELLOW ONIONS, PEELED AND CHOPPED ROUGHLY

6 GARLIC CLOVES, PEELED, SMASHED, AND CHOPPED

1 GREEN BELL PEPPER, SEEDED AND CHOPPED

2 ROASTED RED BELL PEPPERS, PEELED, SEEDED AND
CHOPPED

3 POBLANO CHILES, ROASTED, PEELED, SEEDED, AND
CHOPPED

3 STALKS CELERY, CHOPPED ROUGHLY

1 28-OZ (LARGE) CAN OF BEST QUALITY CANNED
TOMATOES, WITH JUICE

KOSHER SALT AND CRACKED BLACK PEPPER

1 TABLESPOON OLIVE OIL

3 TABLESPOONS ROUGHLY CHOPPED CILANTRO FOR
GARNISH

SHREDDED JACK CHEESE OR CRUMBLED FRESH
MEXICAN CHEESE FOR GARNISH

Skin the chicken breasts and put them in a heavy stewpot. Cover with water. Bring to a boil, then reduce to a simmer and cook 30 minutes or until chicken is almost done. Remove from the pot with a large slotted spoon and allow to cool. When cool enough to handle, strip the meat from the bones in very large pieces and set it aside.

Return the bones to the pot. Add the chicken broth. Cook rapidly until volume is reduced by about one-quarter (this will intensify flavor).

While broth is cooking, heat a wok or heavy dutch oven. Add about 2 inches of oil and heat until a drop of water flicked into the pan sizzles. Add one layer of tortilla strips and sizzle until light gold, then remove with tongs to paper towels. Salt while warm. Strips will continue to color and crisp after removal from the oil. Repeat with all tortilla strips, not crowding the pot. Add more oil if necessary between batches. Strain the bones from the stewpot or remove them with a slotted spoon. Add all the remaining ingredients except the reserved chicken and the garnishes. Cook until vegetables are almost tender, then add the reserved chicken. Taste and check for seasoning. If tomatoes have added a note of bitterness, correct by adding 1/4 teaspoon of sugar. If not spicy enough, add crumbled hot dried red chile or hot red pepper flakes. Add salt and cracked pepper to your taste.

Put a handful of tortilla strips into each diner's bowl. Top with a ladling of soup. Garnish with cilantro and cheese if desired.

Classic Fresh Tomato Salsa

This condiment appears as frequently as a salt shaker on the Mexican and southern Arizona table. Serve with tortilla chips or nachos, or with tamales, carne asada, quesadillas, or marinated meat salads.

3 LARGE JUICY VINE-RIPE TOMATOES, PEELED, SEEDED,
AND CHOPPED

JUICE OF 1 LIME

1 TEASPOON SALT

1 SMALL BUNCH FRESH CILANTRO, CHOPPED COARSELY

1 SMALL SHARP WHITE ONION, PEELED AND CHOPPED

3 SMALL JALAPEÑO CHILES, STEMMED, SEEDED, AND
CHOPPED FINELY

Combine. Allow to sit at room temperature for 30 minutes before serving. Vary the heat by adding or subtracting jalapeños. Correct seasoning to your taste with more salt (or onion or garlic salt) and or lime juice if desired.

Red Chile Sauce

Connoisseurs of chile prefer pure ground red chile (not mixed with other seasonings as commercial red chile powder often is.) Santa Cruz ground chile from Tumacacori, Arizona, and fresh, roasted, or pure ground chile from Chimayo, New Mexico, are excellent choices. Long green chiles (also called Anaheims, New Mexican chiles, or ristra chiles) turn red when they dry. When the late summer harvest comes in the Southwest, the smell of roasting chiles fills the air in many Arizona towns.

Makes about 6 cups.

25 DRIED MEDIUM-HOT OR MILD DRIED RED CHILES

6 CUPS LUKEWARM WATER

6 GARLIC CLOVES, PEELED AND MINCED

1 TABLESPOON OLIVE OIL

1 TEASPOON SALT

2 CUPS CHICKEN BROTH

2 TABLESPOONS UNSALTED BUTTER

2 TABLESPOONS ALL-PURPOSE FLOUR

Preheat the oven to 275°. Wash and dry the chiles. Stem and seed them. Arrange them on a baking sheet in one layer and roast in the oven, turning once, till they are dry but not brown, about 7 minutes. Transfer to a large bowl and cover with the water. Soak 15 minutes. Remove to a colander with tongs, keeping 5 cups of the soaking water.

Purée the chiles with the soaking water in two or more batches in a blender or food processor. Remove to a large heavy saucepan and simmer, uncovered, 20 minutes, stirring frequently.

In a separate pan, sauté the garlic in the oil, then add it to the simmering purée. Set aside the sauté pan. Cook the purée 20 minutes. Add salt and broth. Cook 30 minutes more.

Melt the butter in the reserved sauté pan and blend the flour into it. Cook 2 minutes to make a roux. Scrape the roux into the chile purée. Simmer 10 minutes more to combine flavors.

Skillet-Crisped Quesadillas

This quesadilla method is fast and versatile. Vary the dish by adding other flavors to the filling: roast chicken, spicy cooked sausage, roasted kernels of corn, slivered ham, carne asada, avocado slices, sprouts, roasted red onions, chile sauce (pages 22, 25, 28). Even smoked salmon works! Serves 2 as an entrée or 4 as an hors d'oeuvre.

8 FLOUR TORTILLAS

OLIVE OIL FOR SKILLET-CRISPING

2 TO 3 RED BELL PEPPERS

2 TO 3 ANAHEIM (LONG GREEN) CHILES

FRESH BASIL LEAVES, IF AVAILABLE

A COMBINATION OF CHEESES OF YOUR CHOICE:
GRATED SHARP CHEDDAR, GOOD MONTERREY JACK,
AGED CRUMBLED WHITE MEXICAN CHEESE OR FETA,
OR OTHER FAVORITES GARNISHES

P lace the red peppers and green chiles over a gas flame or under a broiler and roast until charred. Remove to a plastic sack and allow to cool. Peel, seed, and cut into strips. Set aside in two bowls, one for red peppers and the other for the green chiles. Grate the cheese. Cheeses should be varieties that melt easily. If you use feta, which puffs and becomes creamy as it is heated, combine it with a cheese that melts more completely, like Jack.

Heat a heavy skillet and drizzle it with 2 teaspoons of olive oil. Lay one tortilla in the skillet over medium heat. Toast the tortilla for about 2 minutes, then turn it with tongs. Scatter the tortilla fairly thickly with cheese, then chile strips. Add a few leaves of basil. Top with a second tortilla. Toast for 1 to 2 minutes, then lift up a corner to see whether the bottom is beginning to turn golden. When it does, flip the tortilla "sandwich" gently over, using a pancake turner (the cheese will keep the 2 tortillas stuck together). If any filling escapes, scoop it back between the tortillas. Toast again until the second side is golden and the filling is hot and melted. Remove with the pancake turner to a wooden board to cool slightly, then cut into quarters.

Serve with a combination of garnishes: salsa, Green Chile Sauce, Tomatillo Sauce, guacamole or sliced avocados, chopped sharp onion, chopped fresh tomato, chopped fresh cilantro, or other favorites.

26

Spicy Chicken
Enchiladas

The redoubtable corn tortilla is, according to Diana Kennedy, "perhaps the most versatile piece of foodstuff the world has ever known." Serves 4 to 6.

1/2 CUP OLIVE OIL

1/4 CUP CHOPPED WHITE ONION

3 TEASPOONS CHOPPED GARLIC

2 TABLESPOONS FLOUR

1/2 TEASPOON KOSHER SALT

1/2 CUP PURE GROUND RED NEW MEXICAN CHILE POWDER

1 1/2 TEASPOONS GROUND CUMIN SEED PLUS 1 TEASPOON CORIANDER SEED TOASTED IN A DRY SKILLET AND GROUND

2 CUPS RICH CHICKEN BROTH

KOSHER SALT AND CRACKED BLACK PEPPER

2 TO 3 CUPS SHREDDED GRILLED OR ROASTED CHICKEN (OR ROTISSERIE CHICKEN FROM THE SUPERMARKET DELI)

2 TO 3 CUPS COARSELY GRATED EXTRA-SHARP
CHEDDAR CHEESE COMBINED WITH SHREDDED
FLAVORFUL MONTERREY JACK CHEESE
1 LARGE WHITE ONION, PEELED AND CHOPPED
8 TO 12 CORN TORTILLAS
OLIVE OIL

Sauté onion in oil in a heavy saucepan till lightly golden. Add garlic and sauté, taking care not to burn garlic. Add flour, salt, chile, and cumin. Combine. Add 1/2 cup of the chicken broth and stir to make a paste. Transfer to a blender and whirl till creamy, then return to saucepan. Add remaining chicken broth and simmer 30 minutes, adding more broth or water if necessary. Add salt and pepper to taste.

Heat a large heavy skillet and drizzle one teaspoon olive oil in it. Place tortillas in the skillet one at a time, to soften. As each one is softened, remove it to a large platter and fill it with chicken, cheese, and chopped onion. Roll it into a cigar shape and place in a rectangular glass baking dish. Continue until all tortillas are softened, stuffed, rolled, and lying side by side in the dish. Scatter the enchiladas with the remaining onion and cheese. Pour the sauce over. Bake in a preheated 350° oven 25 minutes or until bubbly and golden.

Tomatillo Salsa with Chipotle Essence

Chipotles are smoke-dried jalapeño chiles. At their freshest, they are completely dry but still pliable, brown in color, and possessed of an intensely earthy perfume. Look for chipotles in the Hispanic section of your supermarket or at a specialty store.

Arizona's Spanish roots run deep. The state was part of New Spain, then of Mexico, then of New Mexico Territory before becoming first a territory, then a state on its own. The distinctive (and addictive) Mexican cuisine deftly blends ancient Indian with Spanish influences, plus a dash of French technique (from the brief period of France's dominion over Mexico). A quiet echo of the Moorish past of Spain comes through in some Mexican sweets.

Tart, lemony, little green tomatillos look like very small tomatoes but are quite distinctive in flavor. Tomatillo Salsa is great with crisp tortillas as a dip, dolloped over Sopa de Tortilla con Pollo, with enchiladas, tamales, or quesadillas, or nachos. Makes about 1 cup.

1 DRIED CHIPOTLE CHILE OR ONE CHIPOTLE CANNED IN ADOBO SAUCE IF DRIED ARE NOT AVAILABLE

1 SMALL SHARP WHITE ONION, PEELED AND
   QUARTERED

5 TOMATILLOS, HUSKED, HALVED, AND PARTLY SEEDED
   (SCOOP OUT SOME OF THE SEEDS WITH A
   GRAPEFRUIT SPOON AFTER HALVING TO MAKE THE
   SAUCE SMOOTHER)

5 LARGE GARLIC CLOVES, PEELED

1/2 TEASPOON KOSHER SALT

1 TABLESPOON CUMIN SEEDS, TOASTED IN A DRY
   SKILLET AND GROUND

Scrub the chipotle and place it in a small dish in water to
cover. Microwave one minute (or pour boiling water over
it). It will be puffy as it reabsorbs water. Set aside.

Put the onion, tomatillos, and garlic in a heavy dry skillet.
Toast, turning often, until they are slightly charred in spots.
Garlic will be done first—transfer it to a blender with the
salt. Transfer onion and tomatillos to the blender. Remove the
chipotle from the soaking water, seed, and shred. Set aside.
Pour the soaking water into the blender and add the cumin.
Whirl to combine, but leave a chunky texture. Serve the
shredded chipotle chile separately for those who like it hotter.

O Pioneers!

O ne striking characteristic of Territorial Arizona was its remoteness from other major western settlements. California towns to the west lay mostly along the coast. Utah was sparsely settled, and Santa Fe and Albuquerque were a long way east in the days of travel by horse. Before the era of transcontinental trains, few fresh foods were available except those the pioneers raised themselves. Citrus farming began commercially in the early 1890s in central Arizona. In such an arid place, growing food meant finding water, and the question of who laid claim to that water started early and has continued.

Settlements were established for a handful of reasons. Mormons came to stake new outposts. Miners came to dig silver and copper from the hills at places like Bisbee, Tombstone, and Jerome (named for a New York family who invested in the mines). Nogales grew up as a border town, and Prescott was the early capital. All were small and rough. Even Tucson and Phoenix lacked paved streets until statehood, and statehood came late to Arizona. Only Hawaii and Alaska were slower to add their stars to the flag.

Families coming into the territory by wagon were advised to bring for a 110-day trip "150 pounds of flour; 25 pounds of bacon or pork; enough fresh beef to be driven on the hoof to make up part of the ration; 25 pounds of sugar; and saleratus [baking soda] or yeast powders for making bread."

Ingenious pioneer cooks in Arizona roasted elk and venison, gathered wild purslane for salads, ate cactus buds (high in vitamin C) against the dread scurvy, made jelly from sandhill plums, and when all else failed went hungry.

In military garrisons like Fort Verde, soldiers were issued hardtack biscuits left over from the Civil War (they were still being issued from the same stock during the Spanish-American War). These had to be smashed with a rifle butt and soaked in water for up to a day to be edible. But once soaked, the wallpaper paste-like substance had uses beyond the culinary. It was so adhesive it could also be used to mend horse tack or boots.

Double Apple-and-Buttermilk Pancakes

Apple culture in Arizona began with the settlers and has continued where the altitude is sufficient for enough cold nights while the trees are dormant. Willcox, Arizona, eighty miles east of Tucson, is a center for pick-your-own apple orchards. In Oak Creek Canyon, between Sedona and Flagstaff, the autumn crop of organic apples from Garland's is sold by the roadside. Makes 8 to 10 pancakes.

3 EGGS AT ROOM TEMPERATURE

1 1/2 CUPS BUTTERMILK

2 TEASPOONS VANILLA EXTRACT

1/2 CUP MELTED BUTTER OR MARGARINE

2 CUPS UNBLEACHED ALL-PURPOSE FLOUR

1/2 TEASPOON KOSHER SALT

1 TABLESPOON BAKING POWDER

1/2 CUP SUGAR

1 LARGE FLAVORFUL NEW-CROP APPLE, PEELED, CORED, MINCED

Place the eggs in a mixing bowl and beat until thick. Beat in buttermilk, vanilla, and butter. Set aside. In a separate large bowl, whisk together the flour, salt, baking powder, and sugar. Pour the egg mixture into the flour mixture and fold just to moisten. Fold in apple. Batter will be quite thick.

Drop batter by quarter cupfuls onto a hot, lightly buttered griddle. Allow one side to cook until a few small bubbles begin to rise through the batter at the edges, then flip and cook on the other side. Pancakes will be thick and cake-like.

APPLE TOPPING:

2 FLAVORFUL FIRM APPLES, SUCH AS GRANNY SMITH, PEELED, CORED, SLICED

4 TABLESPOONS DARK BROWN SUGAR, PACKED

3/4 TEASPOON GROUND CINNAMON, MORE TO TASTE

1/4 TEASPOON GROUND NUTMEG

3/4 CUP WATER PLUS 1 TABLESPOON DARK RUM

2 WHOLE CLOVES

1 1/4 CUPS RAISINS

Combine in a heavy saucepan over very low heat and simmer until apples are translucent and liquid is syrupy. Add more water if necessary to keep them from sticking.

30

Spiced Stewed Fruit

As in other parts of the cattle-beset West, the jewel of Arizona's roundup chuckwagon cooks (who reigned supreme on long trail rides) was a canned delicacy: the popular Ottawa Chief tomatoes. Delectability, like beauty, is where you find it.

Canned fruit was also carried on the better-stocked chuckwagons and dispensed as a special treat to saddle-weary cowboys and it was treasured by early settlers on the Arizona frontier. Canned goods have fallen from favor now that fresh fruits are readily available due to long-term cold storage and air transport. However, canned fruits in this compote are even more delicious than fresh. The fruit is good as a side dish with roasted meats or over ice cream. Serves 4 to 6.

1 ONE-POUND CAN PURPLE PLUMS

1 EIGHT-OUNCE CAN PEACHES

1 EIGHT-OUNCE CAN APRICOT HALVES

1 EIGHT-OUNCE CAN PEAR HALVES

4 SLICES LEMON

2 WHOLE CINNAMON STICKS, ABOUT 5 INCHES LONG

SEVERAL GRATINGS OF NUTMEG (OR 1/2 TEASPOON
   PRE-GROUND NUTMEG)

3 WHOLE CLOVES

3 ALLSPICE BERRIES

1/2 TEASPOON DRIED POWDERED GINGER OR 1/4 CUP
   CHOPPED CRYSTALLIZED GINGER OR A FEW SLICES
   FRESH GINGER ROOT, PEELED

1/3 CUP PORT WINE

Drain the syrup from all the fruits into a large, heavy saucepan (but use only half the syrup from the purple plums and discard or save the rest). Put all the fruit in a large bowl.

Add the lemon slices and the spices to the syrup. Boil 20 minutes. Add port to the syrup and pour syrup over the fruit. Return the fruit and syrup to the saucepan and allow to steep for two hours. Heat through before serving.

Sautéed
Chicken Breasts with
Lemon-Rosemary Pan Gravy

Farming became important in Arizona as it grew in the 1800s. Dairy cattle, turkeys, and chicken increased with the human population. In 1888 a few ostriches were brought in from California, and the Salt River Valley was soon the hospitable home to some 6,000 birds, whose feathers were in demand at the time for women's hats. The industry flourished until around the time of the First World War, when styles in hats changed. The eggs were good too. One egg meant supper for the whole family.

Serve with Garlicky Smashed Potatoes (page 57), Baked Polenta Wedges (page 59), rice or pasta and steamed green beans with pine nuts and garlic. Serves 2 to 4.

4 BONELESS, SKINLESS CHICKEN BREASTS

KOSHER SALT AND CRACKED BLACK PEPPER

1/4 CUP FLOUR

1 1/2 TABLESPOONS BUTTER

1 1/2 TABLESPOONS LIGHT OLIVE OIL

1 TABLESPOON CHOPPED FRESH ROSEMARY

2 CLOVES GARLIC, PEELED AND CHOPPED

1 CUP CHICKEN BROTH

2 TABLESPOONS LEMON JUICE

3 TABLESPOONS BUTTER

Generously salt and pepper both sides of the chicken breasts. Dredge in flour, shake, and set aside. Heat a heavy skillet and add the butter and olive oil. When butter begins to color, add the chicken breasts. Cook, without turning, over medium-high heat 4 minutes. Turn and cook the other side 4 minutes more, until crispy and golden. When chicken is done, it will feel firm to the touch and clear juices will begin to appear around it. Remove chicken and keep warm.

Leave the chicken essences, small crispy bits, and oil in the skillet and heat. Add the rosemary and toast slightly. Add the garlic and stir. Add the chicken broth and stir to release all the browned bits into the broth. Add the lemon juice and butter. Taste and add salt and pepper.

Spoon sauce over the chicken breasts and serve.

Apple, Raisin, and Walnut Pie

Apples came to Arizona with the pioneers in the 1800s and they still grow happily in the higher, moister, and cooler areas of the state. Apple pie would have been a fine luxury in pioneer days, and it would likely have been a pie more spare than this one, but it was served in some miners' boarding houses and restaurants as well as in settlers' cottages along Oak Creek where water pumped from the nearby snow-fed stream nourished the early orchards. Serves 6 to 8.

1 TEN-INCH PASTRY SHELL, MADE WITH YOUR FAVORITE PIE CRUST RECIPE, UNBAKED

FOR THE FILLING:

3/4 CUP SUGAR

6 TABLESPOONS FLOUR

1 TEASPOON GROUND CINNAMON

1/2 TEASPOON GRATED NUTMEG

6 LARGE, TART APPLES, PEELED, CORED AND SLICED

JUICE OF ONE-HALF FRESH LEMON

1/2 CUP RAISINS

FOR THE TOPPING:

1/3 CUP SUGAR

1/2 CUP FLOUR

1/2 TEASPOON GRATED NUTMEG

1/2 CUP LIGHTLY TOASTED BROKEN WALNUT PIECES

1/4 CUP COLD BUTTER, CUT INTO BITS

Preheat oven to 425°. Mix sugar, flour, cinnamon, and nutmeg in a large mixing bowl. Add apple slices. Squeeze lemon juice over. Fold in raisins. Pour into pastry shell.

In the same bowl, combine all the topping ingredients except butter. Lightly rub in the very cold butter bits with your fingertips, creating flakes of rubbed topping which will be crunchy when baked. Spread the topping over the pie filling.

Bake 1 hour to 1 hour and 15 minutes. If edges of the shell begin to brown, protect them with a wreath of twisted aluminum foil or a pie crust shield partway through baking.

White Beans with Sausage and Sage

Dried beans, sturdy, portable, filled with protein, were a staple of frontier life. Pork kept better than beef on a long wagon journey or trail ride, and even improved in flavor with aging. Happily, pork was a tasty companion to beans—and still is. Beans could be cooked at night while the pilgrims rested, then eaten cold next day while the family was on the move. Nice with Fresh Corn and Sage Muffins (page 15).
Serves 4 to 6.

2 TABLESPOONS BUTTER PLUS 2 TABLESPOONS
OLIVE OIL
2 CUPS FINELY CHOPPED ONION
2 CARROTS, PEELED AND CHOPPED
4 GARLIC CLOVES, SMASHED, PEELED, AND CHOPPED
1 TABLESPOON FRESH THYME
8 LARGE DRIED SAGE LEAVES OR 2 TABLESPOONS
CRUMBLED DRIED SAGE
1 BAY LEAF
4 CUPS CHICKEN STOCK
1 1/4 CUPS DRIED WHITE BEANS, SOAKED OVERNIGHT,

DRAINED AND RINSED

2 TABLESPOONS OLIVE OIL

1/2 POUND PRECOOKED SAUSAGE SUCH AS
BRATWURST, KIELBASA, PORK SAUSAGE, OR
CHICKEN-APPLE SAUSAGE

Heat the butter and oil in a large, heavy stewpot or Dutch oven. Add onions and carrots and sauté 15 minutes, or until they are almost tender. Add the garlic and sauté another 5 minutes. Add the thyme, sage, and bay leaf. Add the stock and the beans. Bring to a boil, then reduce heat and simmer, partially covered. While the beans are cooking, cut the sausage into small chunks and sauté in the 2 tablespoons olive oil. When golden, remove with a slotted spoon.

When the beans are nearly tender, in about an hour or more, depending on the age and type of the dried beans, add salt to taste and plenty of freshly cracked black pepper. (Adding salt too early in the process makes the beans tough.)

When the beans are tender, add the sautéed sausage chunks to the pot. If there is more liquid than you prefer, ladle part of it out of the pot into a heavy saucepan and cook rapidly over medium-high heat to reduce to a syrupy texture, then return to the pot. This will intensify flavors.

Chocolate Cake with
Arbuckles' Ariosa Coffee

Arbuckles' Coffee, the first pre-roasted bean, was the bev-
erage of choice for Arizona cowboys and Navajo Indians in
the 19th and early 20th centuries. A modern version is avail-
able again from Denny and Patricia Willis of Tucson
(800.533.8278), who have revived the name and the brew.
This sublimely rich cake is not daily fare, but it is well
worth the occasional extravagance. Serves 8 to 12.

1 3/4 CUPS VERY STRONG RICH BLACK COFFEE, SUCH
    AS ARBUCKLES', OR ITALIAN ESPRESSO
1 CUP UNSWEETENED COCOA POWDER (DUTCH
    PROCESS)
2 1/4 CUPS SIFTED ALL-PURPOSE FLOUR
1 1/2 TEASPOONS BAKING POWDER
3/4 TEASPOON BAKING SODA
1/2 TEASPOON KOSHER SALT
1 CUP (2 STICKS) UNSALTED BUTTER, AT ROOM
    TEMPERATURE
2 CUPS FIRMLY PACKED DARK BROWN SUGAR
2 LARGE EGGS
2 LARGE EGG YOLKS

1 TEASPOON VANILLA EXTRACT

1 1/4 CUPS WHIPPING CREAM

1/2 CUP SUGAR

4 LARGE EGG YOLKS

1/8 TEASPOON KOSHER SALT

1 POUND BITTERSWEET OR SEMI-SWEET CHOCOLATE,
   CHOPPED

3/4 CUP BUTTER (1 1/2 STICKS) AT ROOM TEMPERATURE

1/2 CUP LIGHT CORN SYRUP

1/4 CUP SOUR CREAM

Preheat oven to 350°. Lightly butter three nine-inch cake pans. Line the bottoms with waxed paper circles or baker's parchment and butter the paper or parchment.

Put the coffee into a mixing bowl and whisk the cocoa into it.

Sift flour, baking powder, soda, salt. Using an electric mixer, beat the butter until it is fluffy. Add sugar to the butter in four additions, beating well after each. Add the eggs and egg yolks one at a time, beating just to blend after each. Using a large spatula, gently mix the dry ingredients into the butter mixture alternately with the coffee-cocoa, beginning and ending with dry ingredients. Pour the batter into the pans and bake 25 minutes. When slightly cool, turn onto racks and peel off the paper.

For the frosting, combine the vanilla, cream, sugar, eggs, and salt in a large heavy saucepan over medium-low heat and cook, stirring, 7 minutes, or until the mixture coats the back of a spoon thickly enough that you can draw a groove across it with your finger. Do not allow to boil.

Add the chocolate, butter, and corn syrup to the saucepan. Remove the saucepan from heat and stir until the frosting is smooth. Add the sour cream. Refrigerate about 1 hour.

Frost the cooled cakes with the cooled frosting. The recipe makes a very generous amount of frosting; if you do not use it all, it can be refrigerated or frozen for several weeks for another use.

If you're keeping the cake for a few days, refrigerate it because of the sour cream, but serve it at room temperature.

Grilled Leg of Lamb with Juniper Berries and Rosemary

Rosemary grows abundantly in the near-Mediterranean climate of upland Arizona. This recipe, developed by Pat Manhart, pairs its pungent flavor with native juniper to season tender lamb. Serves 4 to 6.

1 SMALL FRESH LEG OF LAMB, SPLIT AND BONED (HAVE YOUR BUTCHER DO THIS, IF DESIRED)

3 TO 4 TABLESPOONS JUNIPER BERRIES

5 CLOVES GARLIC, CRUSHED AND COARSELY CHOPPED

3 TO 4 LARGE SPRIGS FRESH ROSEMARY

3 TO 4 TABLESPOONS OLIVE OIL

FRESHLY CRACKED BLACK PEPPER AND KOSHER SALT

Prepare the grill to medium-high heat. Open leg of lamb butterfly style and pound with a mallet to flatten and tenderize. Scatter the meat with juniper berries, garlic, and rosemary. Pound again to embed the flavorings in the meat. Drizzle with oil and sprinkle with pepper and salt. Grill seasoned side up until meat thermometer registers 180°.

ALL ABOARD FOR ARIZONA!

R ailroads remade Arizona—and its cooking—between 1850 and 1900. The two transcontinental lines that crossed the state, the Santa Fe in the north and the Southern Pacific in the south, revolutionized Arizona's table. Connection to the outer world by rail meant that people, produce, mail, ideas, and raw materials of all kinds could flow from either coast to the inland island of Arizona. By 1912 Arizona had nearly 1,700 miles of railroad track in operation. Without the railroads (sadly, now almost extinct as the passenger pigeon save for a few celebratory short lines) there would have been no Fred Harvey, and without Fred Harvey, there would have been no leap forward in travelers' cuisine in the early days of Arizona.

Harvey meals in the train diner included shirred eggs, silver-domed platters of French toast, aged Kansas City porterhouse, broiled sage hen, rainbow trout, and peach charlotte. Meals at the Harvey Houses established all along the Santa Fe line from Chicago to Los Angeles by the late 1880s were built around the freshest ingredients that could be transported by train from their unthinkably distant origins: oysters, sardines, ripe fruit and lettuce. And they were served by fresh-faced Harvey girls in spotless starched linen cuffs and collars.

As a major means of transport across arid Arizona, the trains would not last. As elsewhere, they were supplanted by private motorized vehicles and a spaghetti-like internet of narrow paved (or, in Arizona, often unpaved) surfaces meant for thoroughfare. But while they lasted, they broke the barrier for food possibilities. No longer could you cook only what you had hauled months on a wagon, rustled up from the brushy environs, traded for with friendly natives, hunted, trapped, or somehow managed to make grow yourself. You could have oysters from Chesapeake Bay. For better or worse, the first step had been taken toward the global village, and the global village had a communal stove.

Train Station
Chicken Salad

Salads, aspics, and fruit cups were civilized fare at Harvey Houses, popular in part because such perishable items had been so hard to come by before the advent of train transport. A Fred Harvey Santa Fe Dining Car Service menu from the early twentieth century displayed an artist's illustration of the El Tovar Hotel on the South Rim of the Grand Canyon in northern Arizona, and beneath it listed, among other offerings, olives, caviar, celery, blue point oysters, milk stew, cold ox tongue, sardines, and chicken salad.

This salad is simple but delicious; vary its flavor with a pinch of your favorite fresh herb (such as tarragon, thyme, rosemary, dill, or chives) and serve on hearts of romaine, or top with raisins, sunflower seeds, and sprouts and serve atop slices of crunchy sourdough toast. Serves 4 to 6.

3 POUNDS WHOLE CHICKEN BREASTS, SKINNED

1 CUP BUTTERMILK OR 1/2 CUP CREAM PLUS 1/2 CUP SOUR CREAM

1/2 CUP GOOD MAYONNAISE

1/2 CUP SOUR CREAM

2 CELERY RIBS, CHOPPED

1/2 CUP WALNUT HALVES, TOASTED LIGHTLY

2 TABLESPOONS CHOPPED PARSLEY

CRACKED BLACK PEPPER AND KOSHER SALT

Place the chicken breasts in a large shallow pan in a single layer. Pour the buttermilk or cream plus sour cream over chicken breasts. Bake at 350° for 25 to 30 minutes, or until done to your taste. Remove from oven. When cool enough to handle, pull meat from the bones.

In a large bowl, whisk together the mayonnaise and sour cream. Fold in the chicken chunks. Fold in celery, parsley, and walnuts. Salt and pepper to your taste and fold again. Cover and refrigerate for 3 to 4 hours to allow flavors to mingle.

Alligator Pear Salad

Avocados have long been appreciated in Mexican cooking and their rich flesh has been called "poor man's butter." (The economy part comes in only if you have your own avocado tree.) Dried leaves from the avocado tree are used in some chicken dishes as bay leaves are in European cooking. When avocados first became familiar north of the border in the 1920s and 1930s, they were called "alligator pears," and appeared as such on early Harvey menus. Serves 4 to 6.

2 TABLESPOONS BALSAMIC VINEGAR

3 TABLESPOONS OLIVE OIL

2 TO 3 DROPS TABASCO SAUCE

PINCH KOSHER SALT

4 RIPE BUT SLIGHTLY FIRM AVOCADOS (TEST RIPENESS BY PRESSING LIGHTLY AT THE STEM END; RIPEN FOR A DAY OR TWO BY PLACING IN A PAPER SACK WITH AN APPLE), PEELED AND SLICED INTO WEDGES

1/2 CUP TOASTED WALNUTS

Combine dressing ingredients and drizzle over avocado slices. Scatter with walnuts. Top with strips of roasted red peppers if desired.

Romaine Spears
with Roquefort and Apples

This appealing combination appeared on an early Harvey menu. Here is a modern rendition. Serves 4.

1/2 CUP ROQUEFORT OR DANISH BLUE CHEESE

1/4 CUP BUTTERMILK

1/4 CUP MAYONNAISE

DASH TABASCO

DASH GARLIC SALT

2 CRISP, TART APPLES, CORED AND SLICED

12 CRISP SPEARS OF HEART OF ROMAINE LETTUCE

Whisk together cheese, buttermilk, mayonnaise, Tabasco, garlic salt. Arrange 3 spears of romaine on each of 4 chilled plates. Dollop cheese dressing over each. Arrange apple slices atop each salad in a fan shape.

Grilled Trout with Saratoga Chips

Saratoga chips, the precursors to today's ubiquitous potato chips, originated according to legend at a resort hotel in Saratoga, Florida. They appeared alongside fish and meat entrées on early Harvey menus. The delicious sauce suggested here is courtesy of Karen Rambo. Serves 4.

1 CUP MAYONNAISE PLUS 1 CUP SOUR CREAM

1 TABLESPOON FINELY GRATED SHARP WHITE ONION

2 TABLESPOONS FINELY GRATED DILL PICKLE

3 TABLESPOONS BRINED CAPERS, UNDRAINED, MINCED

3 TABLESPOONS FRESH LEMON JUICE

1 TEASPOON EACH CHOPPED FRESH DILL, OREGANO, AND THYME (OR 1/2 TEASPOON DRIED)

1 TEASPOON FRESH CHIVES, CHOPPED

1/2 TEASPOON EACH CRACKED BLACK PEPPER AND KOSHER SALT, OR MORE TO TASTE

1/4 TEASPOON SUGAR

3 LARGE, MATURE BAKING POTATOES

VEGETABLE OR PEANUT OIL FOR FRYING

SWEET PAPRIKA AND BLACK PEPPER (OPTIONAL)

4 FRESH TROUT FILLETS

JUICE OF ONE-HALF LEMON

CRACKED BLACK PEPPER AND KOSHER SALT

4 TABLESPOONS BUTTER, IN BITS

SEVERAL SPRIGS FRESH DILL, CHOPPED

Whisk together the first 13 ingredients for the sauce. Add additional increments of any ingredient to taste, then refrigerate so flavors can meld. (Extra sauce keeps well.) Peel the potatoes and slice them as thinly as possible using a mandoline or food processor slicer, or carefully by hand. Put the potatoes in a bowl of ice water. Ideally you should soak them 2 hours, changing the water twice.

Heat oil to 380° for deep frying. Use a deep fryer, following manufacturer's directions, or a deep, heavy pot or wok filled with about 4 inches of oil. Drain and dry the potatoes well. Sprinkle with sweet paprika and black pepper if desired. Fry the chips in small batches until golden. Remove immediately to paper towels and salt lightly while hot.

Sprinkle the trout with lemon, dill, butter, salt, and pepper. Broil or grill the trout until it is golden and can be flaked with a fork (about 5 to 7 minutes per side, depending on

GETTIN' YOUR KICKS ON '66

A rthur Krim, an urban geographer from Newport, Rhode Island, called Route 66 "the symbolic river of the American West in the auto age of the 20th century" along whose course flowed "the American migration from the Midwest to California." On its fabled plunge from Chicago to Los Angeles, 376 miles of The Mother Road cut straight across Arizona.

What became Route 66 began as a link from town to town used mostly by ranchers and Indians. Motor-tourists, Model T adventurers, scientists, and explorers took the road where they could, and its even rougher tributary trails where the road didn't go. Officially named U.S. 66 in 1927, it was not fully paved until the late 1930s.

After World War II, the road took on a new allure as families and the American economy grew, postwar resources were redirected to things like automobile manufacture, and folks

looking to "see the USA in your Chevrolet" turned their eyes to the Golden West.

The Painted Desert, Grand Canyon, the Petrified Forest, Indian reservations, and trading posts beckoned. And enroute to all these places, people had to eat. Increasingly assured a steady flow of traffic, cafés, restaurants, and souvenir shops popped up like soda biscuits along the route during the 1940s and 1950s. Old-fashioned milkshakes, hash browns, pancakes from scratch, meatloaf and mashed potatoes, burgers, steaks, pies, and Mexican specialties lured hungry travelers.

When Interstate 40 gradually displaced the old route, many eateries too far off the new track grew dustier and more vacant, and eventually closed. A rare few survived. With the resurgence of interest in Route 66 in the nostalgic late twentieth century, some are coming back.

• If you feel inspired to look for the road less traveled through Arizona, contact the Historic Route 66 Association of Arizona at P.O. Box 66, Kingman, Arizona 86402, for tips.

Enduring,
Still Wonderful, Meatloaf

Everything changes continuously, of course, but the appeal of long-tested, well made all-American dishes seems to go on. Try this meatloaf with Garlicky Smashed Potatoes (page 57) or Fresh Corn and Sage Muffins (page 15) and "two veg on the side," diner style. Serves 4 with a couple of cold slices left over for a sandwich the next day.

3 TABLESPOONS OLIVE OIL

3/4 CUP CHOPPED SHARP WHITE ONION

1/2 CUP FINELY CHOPPED CARROTS

1/4 CUP CHOPPED FRESH PARSLEY

1/4 FINELY CHOPPED CELERY

1/4 CUP CHOPPED ROASTED SWEET RED BELL PEPPER

2 LARGE CLOVES GARLIC, SMASHED, PEELED AND
CHOPPED

1 TEASPOON KOSHER SALT

1/2 TEASPOON CRACKED BLACK PEPPER

1 TEASPOON GROUND CUMIN

1/4 TEASPOON GROUND CAYENNE PEPPER

3 BEATEN EGGS

1/2 CUP HALF-AND-HALF

1/2 CUP KETCHUP

2 POUNDS LEAN GROUND BEEF

3/4 CUP COARSELY GRATED SOURDOUGH TOAST

Place the olive oil in a heavy, preheated skillet over medium heat. Add the onion, carrot, parsley, celery, and pepper. Sauté until vegetables begin to color, then add garlic and continue to sauté until the mixture is soft. Set aside in a cold bowl to cool.

Place the remaining ingredients except beef and grated toast in a large mixing bowl and combine well. Add the vegetable mixture and blend. Add the beef and grated toast and knead with clean hands to combine well.

Turn out into a buttered loaf pan.

Place the loaf pan in a second larger pan that can hold water up to about half the height of the loaf pan. Pour hot water into the outer pan.

Bake at 375° for approximately 45 minutes.

Chicken-Walnut Burritos

*Burritos are one of those north-of-the-border interpreta-
tions of Mexican food that have been borrowed, slightly bent,
and returned to their cuisine of inspiration. No wonder, as
they are delicious and versatile and can be endlessly revised
to incorporate the whims of the moment. Serves 4 to 6.*

6 CHICKEN BREASTS, STEWED GENTLY IN WELL-
SEASONED CHICKEN BROTH WITH 3 TO 4 WHOLE
CLOVES OF GARLIC UNTIL COOKED, COOLED IN THE
BROTH, SHREDDED FROM THE BONE (DO A DAY
AHEAD AND REFRIGERATE IF DESIRED); RESERVE
ONE CUP COOKING BROTH

3 TABLESPOONS OLIVE OIL

1 TABLESPOON FRESH GROUND CUMIN

1/2 YELLOW ONION, PEELED AND CHOPPED

8 LONG GREEN PEPPERS (ALSO CALLED ANAHEIMS),
ROASTED, SEEDED, PEELED, CHOPPED

KOSHER SALT AND CRACKED BLACK PEPPER

1 WEDGE OF FRESH LEMON, SCRUBBED, CRUSHED AND
DICED (WITH ITS PEEL)

4 TO 6 DASHES TABASCO OR LOUISIANA HOT SAUCE

1/4 CUP VODKA

2 LARGE CLOVES GARLIC, PEELED, SMASHED, CHOPPED

1/2 CUP TOASTED WALNUT PIECES

8 LARGE FLOUR TORTILLAS

1/2 TO 1 CUP SHREDDED MONTERREY JACK CHEESE

GARNISH:

SHREDDED LETTUCE TOSSED LIGHTLY WITH RED WINE
    VINEGAR, SALT, AND PEPPER; RIPE, RED TOMATOES,
    SEEDED AND CHOPPED; CHOPPED GREEN ONION;
    SLICED AVOCADO OR GUACAMOLE

Simmer the reserved cup of cooking broth until reduced by half. Scrape shredded chicken into saucepan with broth and set aside. Add oil to large, heavy skillet and heat. Add cumin and stir. When cumin is lightly toasted and aromatic, add onion, peppers, salt, pepper, lemon, Tabasco, and vodka. Sauté. Add garlic and sauté until it is soft. Add chicken with broth. Cover and steam 5 to 10 minutes. Remove cover and simmer until almost all liquid has been absorbed. Fold in walnuts. Taste and correct seasoning. Preheat oven to 350°. Place a dollop of filling on each tortilla and roll to close. Place closely side by side in an oiled glass baking dish. Scatter with cheese. Place in oven to heat through and melt cheese. Top with garnish.

Green Chile
Cheeseburgers

In Arizona and New Mexico, that roadside staple the cheeseburger gets an Hispanic twist with the addition of roasted green chiles. Serves 4.

1 1/4 POUNDS VERY LEAN GROUND SIRLOIN (PURISTS ADVISE GRINDING YOUR OWN)

1 TABLESPOON CUMIN SEED, TOASTED TILL GOLDEN IN A DRY SKILLET AND GROUND FINE IN A SPICE GRINDER OR MORTAR WITH PESTLE (OR THE BACK OF A SPOON, IF THAT'S WHAT YOU HAVE)

1/4 CUP SOY SAUCE

1 TABLESPOON DRY MUSTARD

4 FRESH LONG GREEN CHILES (ALSO CALLED ANAHEIMS OR NEW MEXICAN CHILES), ROASTED, PEELED, SEEDED AND CUT INTO STRIPS

4 THICK SLICES EXTRA-SHARP AGED CHEDDAR CHEESE

WELL-FLAVORED, CRUSTY SOURDOUGH BUNS OR ROLLS, SPLIT, BUTTERED, AND TOASTED

CONDIMENTS OF YOUR CHOICE

Combine meat with cumin, soy sauce, and mustard and form into patties. Cook to desired doneness in a heavy skillet or on a prepared grill. When almost done, top with strips of chile, then cheese. Cover skillet or grill briefly with a lid in order to encourage the cheese to melt and adhere the chiles to the top of the meat.

Serve on hot toasted buns with your favorite condiments and accompaniments.

Hannah's
Cinnamon Spirals

Breakfast on the road has a special allure. You sleep in a strange bed, your head full of unaccustomed dreams, then rise early and pack up the car. The air, still cool and moist from the night, smells of nearby wheatfields or factories. You go in search of a promising café and find one. The door swings open and you wade into the thick atmosphere: wet wool, smoke, steaming coffee, pancakes on the griddle. A friendly waitress calls you Honey. What could be better? Makes about 18 spirals.

1 PACKAGE ACTIVE DRY YEAST (2 1/4 TEASPOONS)

5 TABLESPOONS WARM WATER

3 TABLESPOONS SUGAR

2/3 CUP CANOLA OIL

2 CUPS BUTTERMILK, AT ROOM TEMPERATURE

4 1/2 TO 5 CUPS UNBLEACHED, ALL-PURPOSE FLOUR

5 TEASPOONS BAKING POWDER

1 TEASPOON BAKING SODA

2 TEASPOONS KOSHER SALT

1/3 CUP FLAVORFUL GROUND CINNAMON OR TO TASTE

1/3 CUP SOFTENED BUTTER

1/3 CUP SUGAR OR TO TASTE

GRATINGS OF NUTMEG

Place yeast in a medium-sized bowl and cover with water. Stir to encourage it to dissolve. Stir in sugar. Stir in oil (it will not blend). Stir in the buttermilk. Set aside.

Put flour, baking powder, soda, and salt in a large mixing bowl and whisk to blend.

Scrape the wet ingredients into the bowl with the dry ingredients and stir just to moisten and combine. Scrape out onto a floured board and knead 6 to 8 strokes. Gather into a ball and place in a warmed bowl. Cover with a clean towel and set aside in a warm place for 30 minutes to an hour (dough will not double but will begin to rise.)

Meanwhile, combine the cinnamon, butter, sugar, and nutmeg into a paste.

Roll out the dough on the floured board very thickly (about 1/2 inch). Spread with the cinnamon paste. Roll up like a cigar. Slice horizontally into rounds. Place rounds on a buttered baking sheet and put into a *cold* oven. Turn the oven to 450°. (Spirals will rise and bake as oven heats.) Bake 10 to 15 minutes.

Banana-Yogurt Pancakes

These pancakes are comfortingly thick. Serve with ham, warmed fruit jam and maple syrup for an at-home diner-style breakfast.

If you are really feeling excessive, add some fresh blueberries and toasted chopped walnuts to the batter, and serve hot Apple Topping (page 30) for triple-fruit pancakes.

Makes about 10 pancakes. Extra cakes can be stacked between layers of waxed paper and frozen, then toasted in a toaster oven for a quick weekday breakfast.

2 CUPS UNBLEACHED ALL-PURPOSE FLOUR

1/2 TEASPOON KOSHER SALT

1 TABLESPOON BAKING POWDER

1/2 CUP SUGAR

3 EGGS, AT ROOM TEMPERATURE

1 CUP MILK OR BUTTERMILK, AT ROOM TEMPERATURE

1/2 CUP MELTED BUTTER OR MARGARINE

1/2 CUP PLAIN LOW-FAT YOGURT, SUCH AS ALTADENA

2 TEASPOONS VANILLA EXTRACT

1 LARGE RIPE MASHED BANANA

Combine flour, salt, baking powder, and sugar in a large mixing bowl and whisk to blend.

In a separate bowl, beat eggs until thick. Beat in milk or buttermilk, butter, and yogurt. Add vanilla.

Pour wet ingredients into bowl with dry ingredients and fold together just to moisten. Fold in mashed banana.

Heat a griddle or large skillet and coat with cooking spray, butter, or oil.

Ladle batter into the skillet (about 3 to 4 tablespoons per pancake). Cook pancakes, turning once when bubbles begin to push their way through the batter and the bottom side is golden. (Batter is thick, so bubbles will be scant.)

Run River Run

A rizona's rivers, the earliest channels of scientific exploration, have become avenues of high adventure, and the rancid bacon and moldy flour John Wesley Powell and his men subsisted on have been replaced by meals of legendary heartiness and savor.

Martha Clark, a seasoned river guide and cook from Flagstaff, says that with state-of-the-art propane stoves, industrial pots and pans, cast-iron Dutch ovens, and giant coolers, river "kitchens" are better equipped than some homes. And, "They certainly have better views. It isn't drudgery to make omelettes for 25 with the music of running water in the back-ground and the morning light creeping down the canyon walls." In spite of the trend toward gourmet everything, including river food, Martha prefers to keep the emphasis in river cooking on the river rather than the cooking, but her outdoor meals are known for their deliciousness.

Use a cast-iron Dutch oven with a flat rimmed lid and legs. Oil it well. Place it out of the wind.

Don't fill the oven too full. A shallower layer of food bakes more evenly. If you are feeding lots of people, use an oven with a wider diameter.

Make sure the charcoal is really hot. Place the Dutch oven over live coals and fill it with food. Mammy Greer adds this tip: Take the diameter of your Dutch oven and multiply by 2. You'll need this number of briquets. Divide this number in thirds and place one-third under the oven and two-thirds on the lid. For example, if your oven is 12 inches in diameter, you need need 24 briquets (12 x 2). 24 divided by 3 = 8. Put 8 briquets under the oven and 16 on top.

Preheat the Dutch oven's lid over a fire or the camp stove. You'll be cooking mostly with heat from the top. After putting the food in the Dutch oven, ring the top of the closed lid solidly with live coals and scatter a few in the center of the lid. This will produce a heat of 350° to 375°—if you don't peek too often.

When it smells great, it's probably done.

• For information about river trips in Arizona, call a good outfitter and agent, such as Rivers and Oceans in Flagstaff, at 800.473.4576 (12620 N. Copeland Lane, Flagstaff AZ 86004), www.rivers-oceans.com, or whitney@infomagic.com.

Martha's Red-Chile Dutch Oven Enchiladas

Providing the wind isn't howling and it isn't raining cats and dogs, you can cook almost anything in an outdoor Dutch oven that you can bake at home. These enchiladas, and river recipes that follow, are specialties that Martha cooks on the river. The best enchiladas, red or green, are made with the best sauce. This dish gets its rich kick from genuine New Mexico pure ground red chile. If you can't find it in stores near you, you can buy it mail order from the Chile Shop in Santa Fe at 505.983.6080 (109 E. Water Street, Santa Fe, NM 87501), www.thechileshop.com, fax 505.984.0737. Serves 8 to 12.

1 CUP UNSALTED BUTTER OR VEGETABLE OIL

6 CLOVES GARLIC, MINCED

1 1/3 CUPS NEW MEXICO PURE GROUND RED CHILE

2/3 TO 1 CUP FLOUR

6 TO 8 CUPS HOT CHICKEN STOCK

2 TEASPOONS GROUND CUMIN

1 TABLESPOON DRIED MEXICAN OREGANO

PINCH OF GROUND CLOVES

KOSHER SALT TO TASTE

3 DOZEN CORN TORTILLAS

2 TO 3 POUNDS MONTERREY JACK CHEESE, GRATED

2 WHITE ONIONS, CHOPPED

4 POUNDS COOKED DICED OR SHREDDED CHICKEN

1/2 POUND FETA CHEESE

In a heavy pan, preferably cast iron, melt the butter and sauté the garlic briefly, not allowing it to brown. Turn the heat to lowest point and add the chile powder. Toast 2 to 3 minutes, stirring constantly. (It burns easily and if it does, it will be bitter.) Add flour and toast another 2 to 3 minutes to create a dry roux. Add hot stock, increase heat, and whisk to desired consistency as it comes to the boil. Add cumin, oregano, and cloves and simmer 20 minutes. Salt to taste.

Meanwhile, deep-fry the tortillas (or fry them in a heavy skillet one at a time in an inch or two of oil). This gives them body and much better flavor.

Prepare the coals for the Dutch oven, using more than usual as you want a hot oven. Oil the Dutch oven. Ladle a layer of sauce into it. Layer tortillas into the pot. Top with more sauce, then add a layer of Monterrey Jack cheese, onions, and chicken. Repeat. Finish with a layer of tortillas, sauce, and then feta cheese. Bake approximately 30 minutes. Let stand 5 to 10 minutes before serving.

Feijoada Grand Canyon

This is Martha Clark's river take on one of the national dishes of Brazil, the feijoada (pronounced fay-zhwah-dah). It is built around two staples of that country, beans and rice, also staples of river cooking. Serves 12.

8 CANS BLACK BEANS

SAUTÉED DICED ONION, TOASTED CUMIN, GARLIC, OR OTHER SEASONINGS TO ENHANCE BLACK BEANS, IF DESIRED (OPTIONAL)

3 TABLESPOONS OLIVE OIL

4 CUPS BASMATI OR LONG-GRAIN WHITE RICE

1 WHITE ONION, PEELED AND CHOPPED

2 TEASPOONS KOSHER SALT

6 RED ONIONS, PEELED AND SLICED INTO ROUNDS

TABASCO, RED WINE VINEGAR, OLIVE OIL

16 BRATWURSTS, ITALIAN SAUSAGES, OR CHORIZOS (OR YOUR FAVORITE SAUSAGE)

16 BANANAS, RIPE BUT FIRM (SLIGHTLY SPOTTED)

UNSALTED BUTTER

BROWN SUGAR

Dress up the beans if you wish and heat. Set aside. Heat 3 tablespoons of oil in a large, heavy skillet or Dutch oven. Add the rice, chopped white onions, and salt. Sauté over low heat approximately 10 minutes. Boil a kettle of water and add a little less than twice as much boiling water as you have rice to the skillet. Return to a boil, then lower heat, cover, and cook over lowest heat for a slight simmer 20 minutes. Let stand 10 minutes before removing lid, then fluff with a fork and set aside.

Immerse the red onion slices in boiling water, then drain. Chill in cold water and drain again. Marinate in equal parts Tabasco, red wine vinegar, and olive oil (approximately 4 tablespoons of each). These are beautiful and will be a hot condiment.

Grill the sausages. Peel the bananas and slice them in half. Fry them in unsalted butter. Add a little brown sugar at the end to caramelize them. Peel and slice the oranges.

Each serving should contain a sausage, a scoop of rice, a scoop of black beans, half a fried banana, some marinated onions, and a slice or two of orange.

Green Chile Posole Stew on the River

Food cooked on the river bank smells and tastes great. No wonder the camp kitchen is the heart of the campsite and the center of warmth and activity. Serves 8 to 10.

1 1/2 STICKS UNSALTED BUTTER

4 LARGE WHITE ONIONS, PEELED AND CHOPPED

6 TO 8 CLOVES GARLIC, SMASHED, PEELED, MINCED

APPROXIMATELY 2/3 CUP FLOUR

10 TO 12 CUPS CHICKEN STOCK (SWANSON'S IF CANNED), HEATED

TWO 28-OUNCE CANS DICED GREEN CHILE

TWO 28-OUNCE CANS WHITE HOMINY

ONE 4-OUNCE CAN DICED JALAPEÑOS (OPTIONAL TO PROVIDE MORE HEAT)

4 TO 6 RUSSET POTATOES, COOKED AND DICED

1 TABLESPOON GROUND CUMIN

1 TABLESPOON DRIED MEXICAN OREGANO

SHREDDED OR CUBED COOKED TURKEY, CHICKEN, OR
PORK (OPTIONAL)
KOSHER SALT AND CRACKED BLACK PEPPER TO TASTE

Melt butter in a large, heavy stewpot or Dutch oven, cast iron preferably. Sauté the onions in the butter for 10 minutes. Add garlic and sauté briefly, until garlic is soft. Turn heat very low and add flour. Toast 2 to 3 minutes. Whisk in hot stock (preheating the stock prevents lumps). Add green chiles, drained hominy, jalapeños (if desired), potatoes, cumin, and oregano and simmer 20 minutes. Fold in cooked chicken or turkey if you are using it just before serving to prevent meat from becoming stringy. Add salt and pepper to taste.

Serve hot with cornbread or quesadillas.

Chile with Pinto Beans, Camp Style

Chopping rather than grinding the meat for this chile dish gives a better flavor and texture. This is a hearty steaming dish for people who have been on the river all day. Serves 10.

1/2 POUND BACON, DICED

3 LARGE ONIONS, PEELED AND DICED

6 TO 8 CLOVES GARLIC, SMASHED, PEELED, DICED

6 JALAPEÑO CHILE PEPPERS, DICED

4 POUNDS CHOPPED BEEF CHUCK OR LEAN STEW MEAT

6 TO 8 CUPS GOOD BEEF BROTH (SWANSON'S IF CANNED)

1/2 TO 1 CUP NEW MEXICO PURE GROUND RED CHILE

2 TABLESPOONS CUMIN

3 TABLESPOONS MEXICAN OREGANO

4 CANS WHOLE COOKED PINTO BEANS

KOSHER SALT AND CRACKED BLACK PEPPER

1 POUND SHARP CHEDDAR OR MONTERREY JACK CHEESE (OR OTHER FAVORITE CHEESE), GRATED

In a large cast-iron pan or Dutch oven, sauté the bacon until it is almost crisp. Add onions, garlic, and jalapeños and cook over medium heat for about 10 minutes.

In a separate pan, sear-fry the meat over high heat. Add it to the onion mixture. Add beef broth, ground chile, cumin, and oregano. Simmer approximately 1 hour. Check to be sure stew meat is very tender and if not continue cooking. When meat is tender, fold in pinto beans gently. Taste and adjust seasonings, adding salt and pepper to your taste.

Serve ladled over fry bread or cornbread and top with grated cheese.

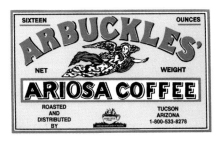

Canyon Cook's
Taco Salad
in Tortilla Packets

Iceberg lettuce is the basis for this "rolled salad" because it keeps well in the coolers on a 10-day trip out. Preserve it whole, not shredded, and don't allow it to freeze. This is Martha Clark's favorite hot-weather lunch for hungry, sun-burned river runners. Serves 10.

- 2 HEADS ICEBERG LETTUCE, SHREDDED
- 1 SMALL JICAMA, PEELED AND DICED
- 1 EACH RED, YELLOW, AND GREEN PEPPERS, DICED
- 4 TO 5 AVOCADOS, PEELED AND DICED
- 1 RED ONION, PEELED AND DICED
- 1 1/2 POUNDS JALAPEÑO-JACK OR SHARP CHEDDAR CHEESE, DICED
- 1 CAN KIDNEY BEANS, DRAINED
- 1 CAN GARBANZO BEANS, DRAINED
- 1 CAN BLACK BEANS, DRAINED
- 1 LARGE JAR GOOD-QUALITY, FLAVORFUL MEDIUM-HOT SALSA, OR HOMEMADE SALSA

4 TO 5 LIMES

PINCH GROUND CUMIN

1 LARGE BAG TORTILLA CHIPS, CRUSHED

12 OUNCES SOUR CREAM

2 DOZEN FLOUR TORTILLAS

ADDITIONAL SALSA

Toss the lettuce, jicama, peppers, avocados, red onion, cheese, and all the beans lightly in a very large mixing bowl. Fold in salsa and chips. Squeeze the limes over the bowl and sprinkle the cumin over. Fold again.

Spoon salad plus a dollop of additional salsa and a spoonful of sour cream into the center of one large flour tortilla and fold or roll to enclose. Repeat until all the tortillas are filled and closed. Serve immediately, with very cold Mexican beer, if desired.

Dutch Oven
Mexican Spoon Bread

This delicious corn pudding is like cornbread, but more delicate, moist, and succulent. It's great alongside barbecued meat or grilled sausages, or with bacon and eggs at breakfast. If you are packing a cooler on the river, you can manage the milk, butter, eggs, and cheese easily enough.

Car-camping or camping with scouts in the wilds of the back garden are also great occasions for this delicious dish.

See Martha's pointers for cooking in a Dutch oven using live coals (page 47). Serves 10 to 12.

2 CUPS STONE-GROUND YELLOW CORNMEAL

TWO 17-OUNCE CANS CREAM-STYLE CORN

1 CUP UNSALTED BUTTER, MELTED

2 CUPS BUTTERMILK

4 EGGS, LIGHTLY BEATEN

1 TEASPOON BAKING SODA

3 TO 4 CUPS MONTERREY JACK CHEESE, GRATED

FOUR 4-OUNCE CANS CHOPPED GREEN CHILE OR
    FROZEN NEW MEXICO ROASTED GREEN CHILES,
    PREPARED AHEAD OF TIME FOR THE TRIP, OR
    FRESHLY ROASTED, PEELED, AND SEEDED LONG
    GREEN CHILES

Start the charcoal for the Dutch oven. Stir together the cornmeal, corn, butter, buttermilk, eggs, and baking soda. Pour half the mixture into the Dutch oven. Add the cheese and chiles in a single layer. Pour remaining batter on top.

Bake approximately 1 hour or until set. Allow to rest 10 minutes before serving.

The New
Southwestern Table

W hat does it all add up to? Tohono O'odham Indians on the Mexican border gathering saguaro cactus fruits. Sixteenth-century Spanish Franciscan monks roasting barbecued kid to relieve the homesick longing for a taste of Old Spain. Early nineteenth-century emigrants bouncing along in wooden-wheeled wagons on dried-mud ruts called roads, conserving their precious flour from St. Louis or Pennsylvania and foraging for edible potherbs among the rabbitbrush. Train passengers on the Santa Fe line in the 1890s amazed that Fred Harvey has somehow managed to provide clean linen and turtle soup. Today's retired CEOs, even in Arizona's much-visited but still little-populated outposts, eating pasta made in Italy.

Upscale Scottsdale restaurants serve roast quail with prickly-pear sauce, French-trained chefs enamored of the chile invent fusion tamales with Asian ingredients. The Southwestern table in America at the beginning of the twenty-first century has been a Johnny-Appleseed to the rest of the nation. Along with the popularity of Southwestern style (Pueblo pottery, clay tiles, Navajo rugs) has come a jolt of surprise for the palate. And the Southwest in turn has welcomed new ingredients.

American taste has grown increasingly adventuresome in the last decades. The pilgrims would be shocked, but salsa is available in supermarkets from Seattle to the Florida Keys and from upstate New York to Baja California.

Culinary experimentation has become characteristic of a country so blessed with plenitude that it can afford to invite flavors and ingredients and food ideas from throughout the world across its borders.

Arizona, a tough, dry land of unsurpassed natural beauty, came late enough to the great table of America to remember foraging and making-do, to respect the hardy indigenous foodways. It's a great place to taste both past and future.

Buttermilk Scones with Red Chile Jam

This combination of traditional European scones with deeply flavored sticky chile jam is delicious.

3 CUPS UNBLEACHED ALL-PURPOSE FLOUR

2 1/2 TEASPOONS BAKING POWDER

1/2 CUP SUGAR

1/2 TEASPOON BAKING SODA

1 TEASPOON KOSHER SALT

1/2 CUP UNSALTED BUTTER, VERY COLD, CUT INTO BITS

1 CUP BUTTERMILK, AT ROOM TEMPERATURE

1/4 CUP HEAVY CREAM, AT ROOM TEMPERATURE

P reheat the oven to 450°. Combine flour, baking powder, sugar, soda, and salt in a large mixing bowl and whisk to blend. Cut in butter with a pastry cutter. Add buttermilk gradually until dough clumps together. (Alternatively, you can place dry ingredients in a food processor and add the butter, whirling just until mixture is sandy in texture. Add the buttermilk in a slow stream, pulsing, until dough clings together at the side of the processor bowl.) Turn out onto a lightly floured board and pat or roll into a half-inch-thick round. Cut into separate rounds with a 2-inch biscuit cutter, or slice the whole round like a pie into sixths or eighths and place on a buttered baking sheet. When almost done, remove from oven and brush tops with cream to create a golden glaze. Bake 15 minutes or until golden.

Red Chile Jam

Sticky, spicy Red Chile Jam keeps well in the refrigerator. Try it with cream cheese and slivered ham on toast as an hors d'oeuvre, or to glaze a hen before roasting. Makes 2 pints.

2 CUPS FRESH RED BELL PEPPERS, SEEDED, STEMMED
    AND CHOPPED
1/2 CUP DRIED RED ANCHOS (DRIED POBLANO CHILES),
    SCRUBBED, STEMMED, AND MOSTLY SEEDED, BUT
    WITH SOME SEEDS AND MEMBRANES FOR HEAT
2 CUPS SUGAR
1/2 CUP APPLE CIDER VINEGAR

Combine in a large heavy saucepan and cook to near the jellying stage. Pour into sterilized jars and seal, or into other containers and refrigerate.

Peppered T-Bones
with Red Wine Sauce

Peppered T-Bones are fast and delicious, with intense flavor. Good with Garlicky Smashed Potatoes, baked sweet potatoes, or cooked root vegetables such as rutabagas, carrots, and turnips, cubed and simmered in salted water till tender.

Serves 4.

1/2 CUP DRY RED WINE SUCH AS MERLOT

1/2 CUP GOOD-QUALITY CHICKEN BROTH

1/2 CUP BEEF BROTH

2 TEASPOONS WORCESTERSHIRE SAUCE

1/2 TEASPOON INDONESIAN SWEET CHILE SAUCE OR
FRUITY BARBECUE SAUCE OR RED CHILE JAM

4 T-BONE STEAKS, TRIMMED OF EXTRA FAT

CRACKED BLACK PEPPER

1/4 CUP BUTTER

Combine sauce ingredients in a heavy saucepan and simmer to reduce to 1/2 cup. Press cracked pepper into both sides of steaks. Add butter to a large flat skillet and heat. Sauté steaks on both sides, about 5 minutes each. Remove with tongs. Add sauce to skillet and cook slightly to achieve glaze-like consistency. Return steaks to skillet and coat with glaze.

Honey-Tequila Glazed Salmon

Try Glazed Salmon with buttery steamed green beans tossed with toasted piñon nuts or steamed asparagus and Polenta Wedges (page 58). Serves 4.

1 3/4 TO 2 POUNDS LARGE FRESH SALMON FILLETS

KOSHER SALT AND CRACKED PEPPER

4 TABLESPOONS TEQUILA

1 TABLESPOON FRESH LIME JUICE

2 TEASPOONS HONEY

3 TABLESPOONS BUTTER, IN BITS

Preheat broiler or grill. Put salmon in a glass dish and rub generously with salt and pepper. Combine tequila, honey, and lime and pour over skinless side of salmon. Allow to marinate 30 minutes. Place salmon in broiler pan skin side down and broil 10 minutes on the second rack down from the heat source until it is golden and flaky, and beginning exude an opaque white essence (or alternatively, cook on the grill). Dab with butter while still hot.

Garlicky
Smashed Potatoes

If any Smashed Potatoes are left over, which is somewhat unlikely, add 2 tablespoons of flour, one beaten egg, and a handful of chopped scallions to each cup of potatoes and spoon into a buttered skillet to make potato pancakes for breakfast.

1 WHOLE HEAD GARLIC

KOSHER SALT AND OLIVE OIL

FLAVORFUL RUSSET BAKING POTATOES, MEDIUM-SIZED, ABOUT ONE FOR EACH PERSON TO BE SERVED

BUTTERMILK

BUTTER, AT ROOM TEMPERATURE

CHICKEN STOCK (HOMEMADE, OR SWANSON'S, IF CANNED)

HALF-AND-HALF OR CREAM

KOSHER SALT AND FRESHLY CRACKED BLACK PEPPER

P reheat the oven to 350°. Slice off the top of the head of garlic to expose the tips of the cloves. Place in a custard cup or small baking dish. Sprinkle with salt and drizzle with olive oil. Cover loosely with foil. Bake 1 hour or until very tender. Baking the garlic makes it sweet and mild.

Meanwhile, peel the potatoes and cut them in quarters. Bring a large pot of well-salted water to a boil and add the potatoes. Cook at a rolling simmer until potatoes are tender. Drain. Return the potatoes to the dry pot and place over low heat. Heat until the potatoes are crumbly-dry and all water is evaporated from the pot, shaking it to prevent sticking (very dry potatoes absorb more flavor and mash more easily).

Put the potatoes into a large mixing bowl. Squeeze the garlic pulp out of the cloves into the potatoes—use as much of the garlic head as you wish. (Any portion not used can be added to soups or sauces, or mixed with butter for garlic toasts.)

Mash with a potato masher. Add buttermilk, softened butter, chicken stock, and half-and-half or cream in approximately equal proportions, continuing to mash, until the potatoes are the consistency you prefer. Season to taste with salt and pepper.

Pork with Green Chile and Olives

Strange as it seems to consider Arizona Mexican cooking without beef or pork, cattle and pigs did not arrive in what is now Arizona until sometime after they were imported to Mexico by the Spanish. This make-ahead dish has deep, intense flavor. It cooks a long time, but requires little attention after you put it in the pot. Serves 4 to 6.

2 TO 3 TABLESPOONS OLIVE OIL

1 WHITE ONION, PEELED AND COARSELY CHOPPED

4 VERY THICK, MEATY SLICES PORK SHOULDER CUT
COUNTRY-RIB STYLE

3 CLOVES GARLIC, PEELED AND CRUSHED

2 TEASPOONS CUMIN SEED, TOASTED IN A DRY SKILLET
AND CRUSHED, OR GROUND CUMIN

KOSHER SALT AND CRACKED BLACK PEPPER

1 RIPE TOMATO, PEELED, SEEDED, AND SPRINKLED
WITH A LITTLE OIL AND VINEGAR

1/2 TO ONE RIPE RED PEPPER, ROASTED AND PEELED,
SEEDED AND CHOPPED

ONE RECIPE GREEN CHILE SAUCE (PAGE 22) — ABOUT 2
  CUPS OR TO TASTE
2 TO 3 CUPS GOOD CHICKEN BROTH
1/2 TEASPOON SUGAR
1/2 CUP GREEN OLIVES

Put the olive oil in a Dutch-oven or heavy tall-sided skillet. Sauté the onions. Add the pork pieces and brown on both sides. Add garlic, cumin seed, salt, pepper, tomato with soaking vinaigrette, red pepper. Sauté. Add Green Chile Sauce and broth. Add sugar.

Simmer the dish for 2 to 3 hours or until pork is extremely tender and is falling off the bones. Add olives when you think it's about 45 minutes from being ready to serve. Add additional broth if necessary. If it's too liquid at the end, ladle out a saucepan full of the sauce and cook separately over high heat to caramelize and reduce (you can put the olives in this saucepan if you haven't added them yet), then return this to the mother dish. (This is a great way to intensify the flavor if you have the time to do it.)

Before serving, remove the bones and break up the pork into generously sized, tender chunks with a spoon. Correct seasoning for your taste and ladle over Baked Polenta Wedges.

Baked Polenta Wedges

How appropriate to begin and end the recipes in this book with corn, the staple of the Southwest. Polenta Wedges are great for soaking up rich juices of a meat entrée, or for breakfast with ham and eggs. Makes 6 wedges.

1 CUP STONE GROUND CORN GRITS OR POLENTA

2 CUPS GOOD CHICKEN BROTH (OR CANNED GARLIC-
FLAVORED CHICKEN BROTH, SUCH AS SWANSON'S)

1 CUP WATER

1/2 TEASPOON SALT

1/2 CUP SHREDDED CHEDDAR OR ASIAGO CHEESE

Bring the water and broth to a boil. Sprinkle in the polenta, stirring, very gradually, over medium heat. Cook about 5 to 15 minutes, until all the polenta or grits are incorporated. Remove from heat and stir in the cheese.

Pour this into a buttered pie pan and place in a preheated 350° oven. Bake about 20 minutes. Slice pie-wise and serve. Allow to set just a little so you can cut it into nice wedges.

Index

59

60